All About Whales

By Roy Chapman Andrews

Former Director, American Museum of Natural History

Illustrated by Thomas W. Voter

RANDOM HOUSE
NEW YORK

This book is for
Dena
and for
John Moore Shaul

SIXTH PRINTING

MANUFACTURED IN THE U.S.A.

LIBRARY OF CONGRESS CATALOG CARD NUMBER: 54-7001

Contents

1.

My First Whale Hunt

"Whales on the port bow!" The cry rang from stem to stern of the whaler *Orion.*

I jumped as though a bomb had exploded and grabbed my camera. The shout had come from the man standing in the barrel at the masthead with field glasses at his eyes. He was watching for whales in every direction. I was on my first whale hunt and was eager to see everything, but the whales were still a long way off. The Captain tried to show me the spouts. Finally I could see the columns of vapor shooting fifteen feet into the air. I got out my notebook, pencil and stop watch. There were three whales—all humpbacks. They blew five times at intervals of thirty seconds. This got their great lungs well filled with fresh air. Then, as if at a signal, the three black bodies slowly rounded into view. The propeller-like flukes were smoothly lifted out of the water and gradually disappeared below the surface. It is impossible to describe the ease and beauty of the dive. The humpback whale has a thick, heavy body and long, ungainly flippers. You would never think there could be grace in any movement. Yet the enormous animal slides beneath the surface as smoothly as a water bird.

"Those whales aren't feeding," Captain Balcom said. "When they bring out the flukes, it means a deep dive. We call it 'sounding.' No telling where they'll come up next."

By my stop watch the humpbacks were down seventeen minutes. They rose for two spouts and dove again. The Captain rang for full speed ahead. Soon we were on the mirror-like patches of water left by the whales where they went down.

After ten minutes three silvery clouds suddenly shot into the air. They were a quarter of a mile away. Instantly the engine signal rang. The ship ploughed ahead at full speed until the whales sounded.

For two hours this went on. Several times we were almost near enough to shoot. Then the big fellows would arch their backs and turn down in a beautiful dive. The great flukes seemed to wave at us in scorn.

I kept my notebook and pencil at work as well as the camera. It was difficult to use either. The wind had risen, and I was deathly sick. Even the best sailors lose their "sea legs" on one of these little round-bottom vessels. The *Orion* twisted and writhed about like a wild thing. She would climb a huge wave, rock uncertainly a moment on the crest, and then plunge headlong down its smooth, green slope. I was certain she would never rise again.

Captain Balcom hung on to the harpoon gun. I stood just behind him with my arm about a rope. After we had been soaked by a big sea, he shouted, "If we don't get a shot soon, we'll have to leave them."

We were heading for the whales spouting only a short distance away. One of them had left the others and seemed to be feeding. He was swimming at the surface. Sometimes he went under for a few seconds but never far down. The ship slid nearer and nearer with engines

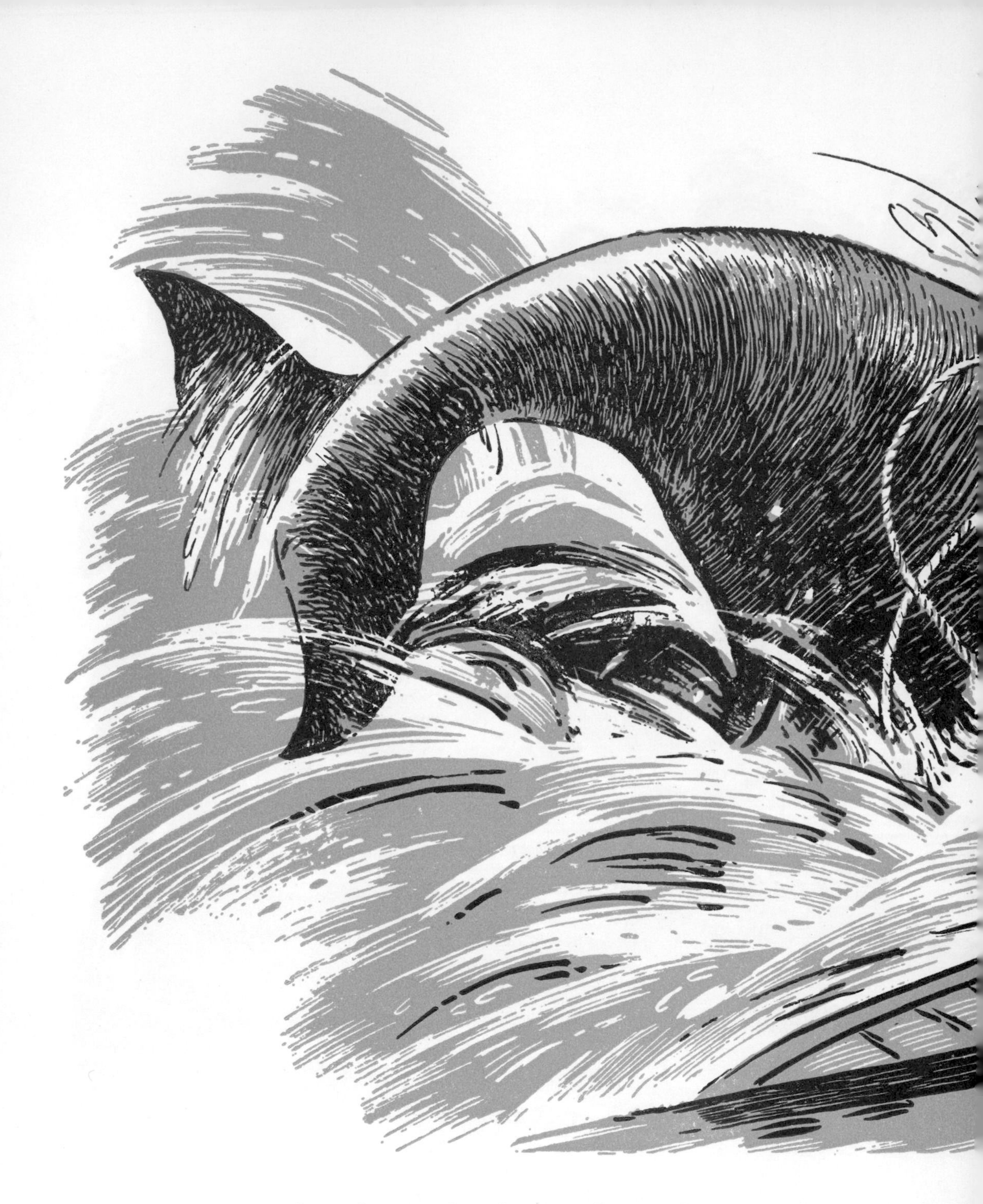

I caught a glimpse of a phantom shape rushing upward.

Instantly came the deafening roar of the harpoon gun.

at dead slow. The whale disappeared just out of range. "In a minute he'll come again," shouted Balcom. "Get ready." He was bending over the gun, feet braced.

I clung to the rail, trying to focus the camera. Flying spray made it almost impossible. Suddenly the Captain's muscles tightened, and the tip of the harpoon dropped an inch or two. I caught a glimpse of a phantom shape rushing upward. A second later an underwater volcano seemed to explode. A great body burst to the surface, and a blinding cloud of vapor shot into our very faces. Instantly came the deafening roar of the gun. I saw the great black flukes whirl up and fall in one tremendous, smashing blow. Then the whale straightened out, rolled on its side and sank.

For minutes absolute silence hung over the ship. Everything seemed poised and motionless. Then the men quietly went about their work. Balcom leaned over the side. The rope hung straight down from the bow, rigid as a bar of steel. "The harpoon hit him right in the heart," he said. "It killed him instantly."

I sat down on the gun platform, weak from excitement. I was half dazed too. I hadn't expected anything like that. It was terrifying! The whale seemed like some dreadful prehistoric monster rising out of the sea to swallow the ship! The black dripping body, the crashing roar of the gun, and the great flukes waving in the air! It was like a nightmare!

That humpback was the first live whale I had ever seen. I have never forgotten him. It took several such experiences before I could get used to it. After a while I knew what was going to happen and could prepare myself. But it was always tremendously exciting.

When the Captain was sure the whale was dead, he shouted to the engineer to reel in the line over the winch. Fathom after fathom came in. (A fathom is

For the return trip the whale was lashed to the side.

six feet.) The little vessel heeled far over under the great weight. I clung to the rail, looking down into the water. Soon the shadowy outline of the whale, with flippers widespread, neared the surface.

Two sailors rigged a long coil of rubber hose. One end was attached to an air pump, the other to a spear-pointed tube of steel. This was jabbed into the whale's stomach, and the pump started. Slowly the body filled with air. When it floated easily, the tube was withdrawn. Then the hole was plugged with oakum. With a heavy chain the sailors made the whale fast to the bow of the ship, tying it tail first.

The other humpbacks were a long way off when we were ready to start. The man in the barrel reported them to be traveling fast. There was little chance of getting another shot. Moreover, the wind was blowing half a gale. So the Captain decided to run for the station. It was one-thirty in the morning when we came into the calm waters of Barkley Sound, which cuts a deep gash in the heart of Vancouver Island.

2.

The Land Animal That Went to Sea

Even though whales live in the water, they are not fish; they are mammals. Mammals have warm blood that remains at the same temperature all the time. The blood of a fish is "cold" and changes with the temperature of the water. Mammals breathe air with lungs. Fish breathe oxygen in the water by means of gills. The young of fish are hatched from eggs. The young of mammals are born alive and nursed with milk. A whale's milk is white and looks just like cow's milk.

The great, many times great, grandfathers of whales lived on land. That was fifty or sixty million years ago. No one knows just how long. But we do know they are one of the oldest groups of mammals. When they lived on land, they had bodies like other mammals. They were covered with hair, walked on four legs and had ears on the outside of their heads.

For some reason the ancestors of whales left the land and took up life in the water. We can only guess *why* they did that. But we can see *how* it was done if we look at a seal. The ancestors of seals used to be entirely land mammals, but many years ago they began to spend more and more time in the water. Now they only come out on the shore to give birth to their young and to sleep in the sun. Their bodies have changed a great deal to fit them for life in the water. After a few more million years they will undoubtedly become as fishlike in shape as whales and never come on land. Whales must have gone through the same stages that seals are going through.

Nature did an amazing job in adapting a whale to live in the water. One would never think it was possible. Everything about the body, inside and out, had to be changed. It was a very, very, very slow process. Millions of years passed before the change was complete.

To be able to move through the water easily, the body must be long and slender. So in each generation of the ancestral whales, the body grew to be more and more like that of a fish.

Any part of an animal that isn't being used disappears eventually. That is why whales have no external ears. Outside ears help a land mammal to collect the sound waves that pass through the air. You have often seen a partly deaf man put his hand behind his ear to help him hear. But water carries sound much better than air. Therefore, outside ears are not necessary to a whale or any other animal that lives in the water. A whale's ears show only as a tiny hole on each side of the head behind the eye. But the muscles that used to control the outside ears are still there under the skin. So we know whales once had external ears. The ears of seals are tiny and are gradually disappearing. In generation after generation the ears get smaller as the animals spend more and more time in the water and less on land.

Nature had to make an extraordinary change in the way a whale breathes. Because it is a mammal, a whale must hold its breath below the water's surface just like a person. If it didn't, it would drown.

A whale must breathe as soon as possible when it

comes up from a long dive. So Nature moved the nostrils backward and up to the very top of the head. Thus the nose is the first part of the body to appear when the whale rises to the surface.

As soon as a whale reaches the surface, it opens its nostrils. These have been closed as tight as a trap door. The whale blows out its breath in a great *whoosh*. The breath has become hot from staying in the lungs for such a long time. Also it is saturated with water vapor.

When it strikes the cool outer air, it condenses and forms a column of vapor. You can do the same thing on a cold winter day when you "see your breath." The whale's vapor column shoots up fifteen or twenty feet. Whalemen called it the "spout."

People used to believe that whales took water in through the mouth and spouted it out through the nose. A whale could not do that because of another adaptation that Nature has made. The nasal passages do not open into the back of the mouth as in a land mammal. Instead they are directly connected with the lungs. This is by means of an extension of the windpipe, called the "epiglottis." It fits into the soft passage between the nostrils and the lungs. It entirely shuts off the nasal tubes from the mouth. Thus the whale can swallow its food beneath the surface without getting water in its lungs. But it can't breathe through its mouth.

There are two big classes of whales. The baleen, or whalebone, whales make up one group. The toothed whales and porpoises make up the second. On the following chart, you can see just how the various kinds of whales fit into these two groups or classes.

Baleen or Whalebone Whales

Fin Whales or Rorquals (Back fin, short baleen, throat folds.)

Humpback whale	Sei whale
Finback whale	Little piked whale
Sulphurbottom whale	Bryde's whale

Right Whales (No back fin, long baleen, no throat folds.)

Right whale	Pigmy right whale (Back fin, long baleen, no throat folds.)
Bowhead whale	

Gray Whales (No back fin, short baleen, 2 to 4 throat grooves.)

Toothed Whales

Sperm whales	Porpoises
Beaked whales	Fresh-water porpoises

The toothed whales and porpoises have teeth and eat squid and fish. Since none of them chew their food, the teeth are all alike. They are peglike and well suited to holding slippery fish. The teeth vary in number in different species. The sperm whale, which is the largest, has twenty to thirty big teeth. Some other whales have

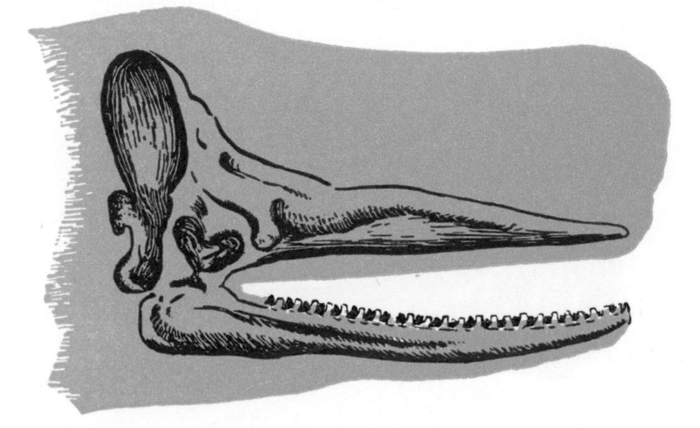

The teeth and jawbones of a toothed whale are shown in black.

only two or three. But the narwhal that lives in the Arctic has a single tooth. It has developed into a great tusk seven or eight feet long.

Millions of years ago all the baleen whales had teeth and probably ate fish. But for some unknown reason they changed their feeding habits. They began to eat smaller and smaller things. They particularly liked crustaceans (crus-TAY-shuns) such as shrimp. Teeth were of no use in getting these tiny animals so Nature took care of it by producing a most extraordinary growth in their mouths. This is called baleen or whalebone.

Land mammals have cross ridges in the membrane of the roof of the mouth. In baleen whales these ridges have become greatly enlarged into a series of flat plates

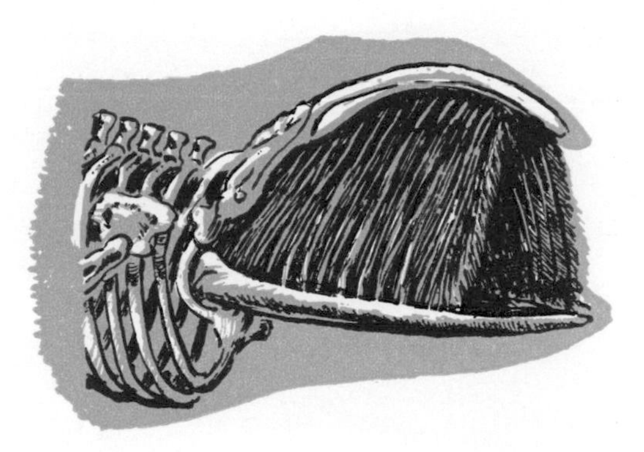

This shows the skeleton of a baleen whale's head in black.

of *keratin,* the same substance your fingernails are made of. The plates hang side by side in the upper jaw where teeth would normally be. The inner edge of each plate is frayed out into bristle-like hairs that form a thick mat. The whale takes in a mouthful of water containing thousands of shrimp. As he shuts his mouth, the huge flabby tongue squeezes out the water between the plates. The shrimp are strained out by the hairlike mat.

Baleen is usually called "whalebone." That term is not correct since baleen is a skin growth and has nothing to do with bone.

No specialization for the securing of food is more remarkable than the whale's baleen. It is almost unbelievable that Nature could replace teeth with such a complicated straining apparatus. But we know baleen whales once did have teeth. Tiny teeth are still present in the mouths of unborn young. They disappear before the baleen develops.

When whales began to live entirely in the water, Nature had to provide some way to keep them warm. A fish doesn't have to worry about that, for when it is cold the blood temperature of a fish drops. In warm water it rises. But a mammal's blood always remains at the same temperature. A dog or a cat or a bear grows longer and thicker hair in the winter. That prevents the body heat from being absorbed by the cold air. People do the same thing by putting on more clothes.

Nature solved the problem of keeping the whale warm by developing a thick layer of fat, called "blubber," between the skin and the flesh. Fat makes a very warm blanket. Whales that live in the cold Arctic seas have very thick blubber. The blubber of those species that inhabit temperate or tropical waters is comparatively thin.

Seals have blubber too. It is not very thick since they also have fur or hair. That is because they live partly on land. After some millions of years, when they come to spend all their time in the water, the hair will vanish. Then the blubber will be much thicker. The walrus of the Arctic Ocean has thick blubber and its hair is thin.

The ancestors of whales were once entirely covered with hair. Since it is no longer needed, it has mostly disappeared. But the baleen whales still have a few short, stiff hairs scattered over the chin, nose, lips and on top of the head.

Besides giving warmth to a land mammal, hair acts as a protection for its skin. But a whale doesn't need hair

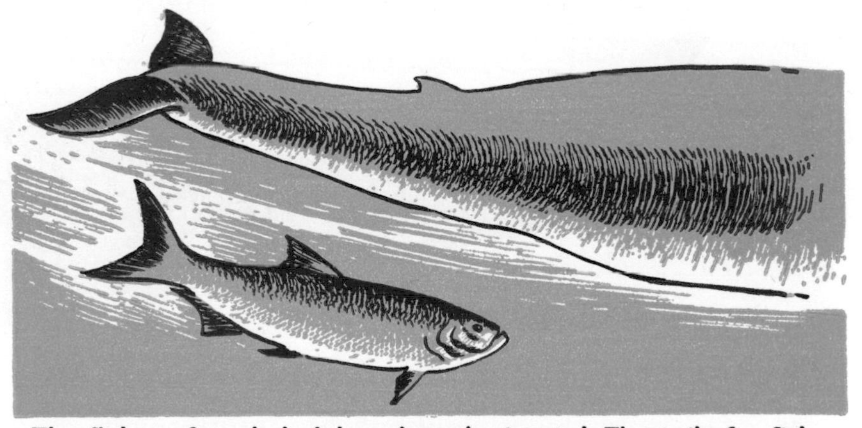

The flukes of a whale (above) are horizontal. The tail of a fish (below) is vertical.

for that purpose even though its skin is very soft and thin. Because it lives in the water, it doesn't have to worry about thorns or bushes or rocks which might tear its skin. A big whale has skin only half an inch thick. It is perfectly dry and has no oil or sweat glands. They proved to be unnecessary so they disappeared.

When whales took to the water, they had to have some way of swimming well. Thus the back part of the body expanded. It became the wide, flat, boneless tail, or "flukes." The tail of a fish is vertical, but the flukes of a whale are horizontal. The flukes help the whale to rise to the surface quickly.

The legs of a land mammal are not wide or flat enough for good swimming. So the bones and fingers of the

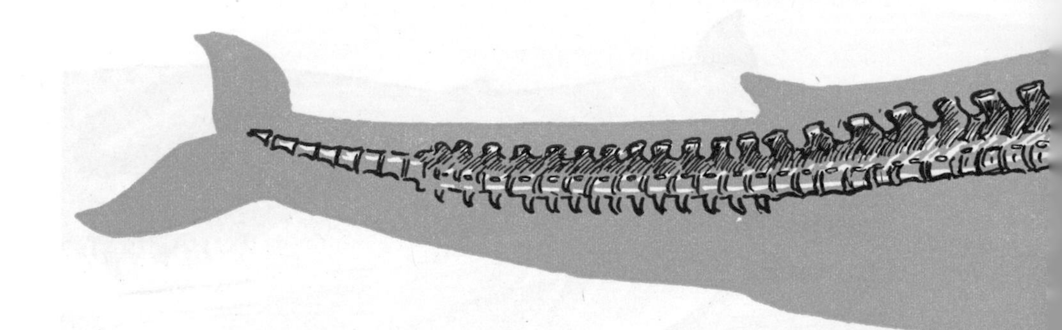

The skeleton of a whale is very loosely jointed.

whale's forelegs grew together. After a while they became covered with connective tissue and blubber. These make very fine paddles. They help in rapid turning and in balancing while the flukes push the whale forward. Because the hind legs weren't of much use, they became shorter with each generation. After millions of years they disappeared entirely. In living whales the only remnants of these hind legs are small chunks of bone buried deep in the flesh. (See picture on page 38.)

The changes that had to be made inside the whale are just as remarkable as those on the outside. The entire skeleton is loosely put together. Thus the animal's body is very flexible and has great freedom of movement for swimming. To support the big head the bones of the

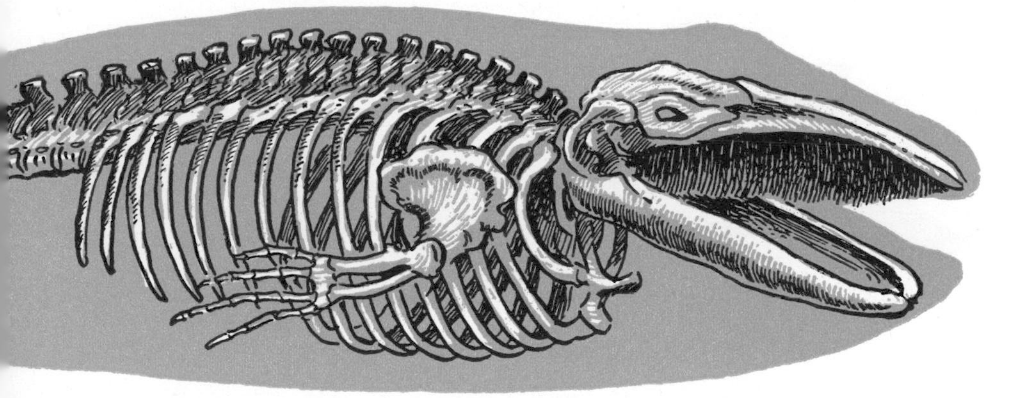

The neck bones are short and placed close together.

neck are shortened and packed close together. The breastbone is very small. The ribs are so loosely joined to the backbone that the lungs can be completely filled with air.

Whales are the biggest animals that ever lived. Why can they grow so large? It is because the water supports their bodies. If a land animal gets too big, its legs can't hold it up and it is unable to move about. If a bird is too heavy, it cannot fly. But there is no limit to the size a whale can grow since water supports it.

For this same reason the young whales are very large at birth. I saw a new-born sulphurbottom whale that was twenty-five feet long. Its mother measured eighty feet. The baby weighed about 16,000 pounds. A land mammal could not carry babies of such size.

All whales live in oceans. Most of the porpoises do, too, except for one group found in the Ganges River, the Orinoco River and the Tungting Lake of China.

No example of evolution is more wonderful than that of whales. But it must be remembered that this extraordinary change from a land to a water mammal was very slow. In each generation the body structure was altered a little more to fit the new life. It took millions of years to produce a whale as we see it now.

3.

Whaling Through the Years

The quest for gold was the greatest reason for the early exploration of the earth. Next to gold came the search for new whaling "grounds." Whaling was of vital importance, too, in the economic history of the Old and New Worlds. In no other industry is there such a wonderful story. Since earliest times it has been a history of romance, danger, hardship and adventure. Even in the twentieth century the story continues. It is a different story, but it is still exciting.

The value of whales was first shown to people living along the Mediterranean Sea nearly a thousand years ago. The Basques, who lived on the coast of Spain in the Bay of Biscay, found a dead whale on the beach. They discovered that its fat blubber gave quantities of oil which they needed for dip-lamps in their church services. So they began to think of getting more whales. At that time hundreds of whales of different kinds came into the bay. The Basques started to hunt them. But they soon learned that a certain species yielded more oil from the blubber than any other. Moreover, it was easier to kill and did not sink when dead. So they called it the "right whale to kill." Ever since then the animal has been known as the "right" whale.

As years went by, whales ceased coming into the Bay of Biscay. So the hunters ventured farther out to sea in their search. Eventually they turned northward. In the waters near Greenland they found another kind of whale. It was much like the right whale but larger. The head was one third of its entire length. It was arched almost in a half circle. The baleen was ten to fourteen feet long and the blubber fifteen inches thick. The animal became known as the Greenland right whale or bowhead.

By the end of the sixteenth century, the Basques had sailed as far as Iceland, Newfoundland and Labrador in their search for whales. Ships of America, Holland, England, Germany, Denmark and Norway were also hunting whales.

Right whales and bowheads were the only kinds of whales hunted for many years. But at the beginning of the eighteenth century, sperm whales became the basis of the American industry. The sperm is a strange looking beast, fifty or sixty feet long. Instead of baleen it has a narrow jaw armed with big cone-shaped teeth. The blubber is very thick and gives much oil. In the great head it has an oil tank containing spermaceti, a very fine oil, which can be dipped out with a bucket. Sperm whales do not sink when dead.

In the early years whale hunters made long voyages into distant oceans. Then ships were small, the dangers great and the waters unknown. The sailors faced lonely months and years away from home. They were often shipwrecked. But they discovered new lands and charted new seas. Those whale hunters were great explorers.

The years from 1635 to 1860 made up the great period of the American whaling industry. In 1846 more than 735 whaling vessels sailed out of New Bedford,

Often the whale swam away towing the boat with it.

Nantucket, Provincetown and other New England ports.

New England whaling ships were of good size. Each carried several small boats. When a whale was sighted, one or two boats put out from the ship. A boat was rowed or sailed close to the whale. As the animal came up to breathe, a hand harpoon was thrown into its body. This was called "getting fast." The harpoon carried a rope attached to the boat. The whale would dive and swim away towing the boat after it. Sometimes the pace was so fast that the whalers called it a "Nantucket sleigh ride."

When the whale tired a little, the boat would steal up very quietly from behind touching the animal's side. The sailors called this "wood to black skin." Then the ship's mate thrust a long, slender lance into the whale's lungs. The boat backed off quickly, for that was the dangerous time. The tail, or flukes, went up and then came down with a terrible blow. Sometimes the boat was hit and smashed to kindling wood. Sometimes the men were killed.

The dead whale was towed to the ship where it was "cut in." That means stripping off the blanket of blubber while the carcass rolled over and over in the water.

On deck the blubber was sliced into pieces and boiled in big kettles to "try out" the oil. This was poured into barrels and stored in the hold of the ship. After the blubber was off, the body was left to the sharks.

If a ship was successful in finding whales, it might return to its home port in six months or a year. But sometimes the cruise would last two or three years. When a whaler sailed away, friends shouted, "A short voyage and a greasy ship!"

By the end of the Civil War the American whaling fleet had been almost destroyed. But just at that time a Norwegian, Sven Foyn, invented a harpoon gun. This is a short cannon shooting a bomb harpoon. It is mounted on the bow of a small steamship.

The harpoon has a double shaft and four long barbs at the end. It is tipped with a hollow point called the "bomb." This is filled with powder. Three seconds after the gun is fired, the bomb bursts. Pieces of iron are thrown in every direction. Often a whale is killed instantly.

A large ring slides along the double shaft of the harpoon. To it is fastened a heavy rope which runs backward over a double winch and down into the hold of the ship. By means of the winch, a whale is "played" as a fish is played by the reel on a fishing rod. If the whale dashes off, some of the line is dragged out. When it stops, the winch pulls in as much as it can get before the animal takes another rush. Usually more than a mile of rope is carried.

The harpoon gun ship is operated from a station on shore. The whales are brought to the factory where the oil is boiled out from the blubber and the flesh and bones made into fertilizer.

The first shore stations were established on the coast of Norway. Business was so successful that it spread to other parts of the world. In 1915 eighteen whaling factories were operating from Newfoundland. Thence the industry went to the Pacific coast: Vancouver Island, Alaska and California. Russians and Japanese started operations along the shores of Siberia, Korea and Japan. Also it spread to South Africa, New Zealand and the islands of the Antarctic Ocean. South America had stations on the coast of Brazil, Argentina and Chile. It rapidly became a world industry.

When whales began to get scarce near shore, the "floating factory" was invented. This is a large steamship which is fitted with boiling vats. It can move from place to place as the whales travel. The dead whales

Sometimes the boat would touch the great whale's side.

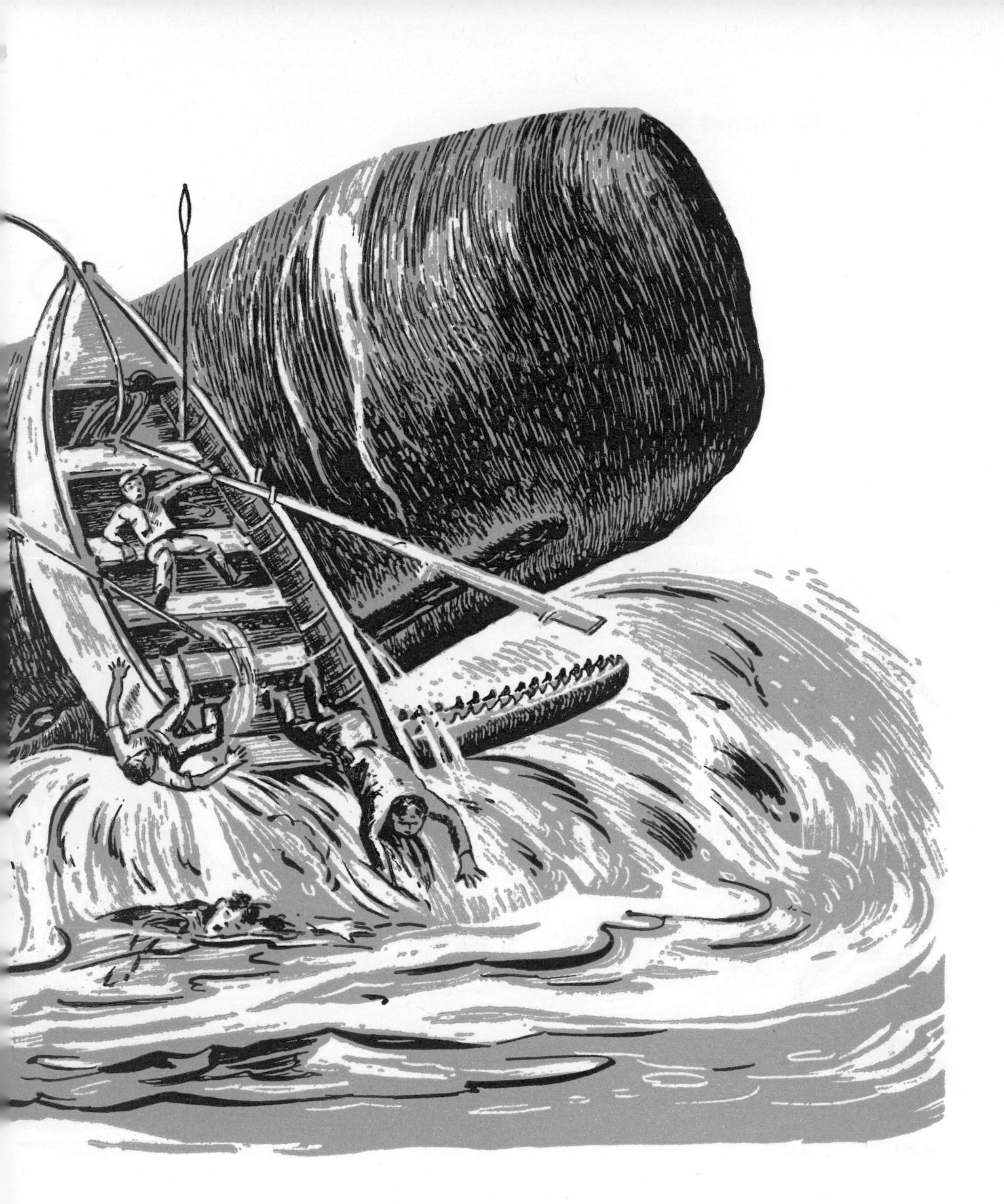

Sailors used to call this "wood to the black skin."

are pulled into the stern of the ship by a steam winch. There they are cut up. The floating factories are mostly used in the Antarctic where there is the greatest number of fin whales.

Whaling is big business today as it has been for many centuries. Much money is invested. Now that whale oil can be refined, it is an important food product. Some people, like the Japanese, eat the meat. Their First Fleet of the 1947-48 Japanese Antarctic Whaling Expedition numbered twelve ships. They had the factory ship where the whales were cut up, two ships for salting and freezing the meat, two cold storage vessels, six catcher ships and an oil tanker. There were 1300 Japanese employed in the fleet.

Other nations have heavy investments in whaling too. Therefore, it has been necessary to make proper international laws so the whales will not all be killed off. To do that, nations had to know the real truth about the habits of whales.

The British Government formed the Discovery Committee to study the habits and life history of whales. They built a ship, the *William Scoresby*, to follow whales and mark them. In this way they could find out where the animals went and when.

During the seasons from 1934-35 to 1937-38, the *Scoresby* marked 5000 whales in Antarctic waters. A ten-inch stainless steel tube, with a paper inside, was shot into each whale's blubber. It did not hurt the animal. If the whale was killed later, the tube was easily found during the cutting in. It offered a reward to anyone who returned the record. On it were questions about where and when the whale was taken. The answers were sent to the Colonial Office in London where the information was studied. In this way much has been learned about the routes whales travel. It is no longer so much guesswork as it used to be.

Whales are always on the move and travel over great distances. The word "migration" is used to mean the yearly long journeys from warm to colder waters.

It was learned that various groups, or communities, of whales exist in the Northern and Southern Hemispheres. Each group has a regular migration route. The sulphurbottom and other fin whales of the Southern Hemisphere arrive in the ice-filled Antarctic Ocean in November and December which are summer months there. They travel fast when migrating. A marker shot into one sulphurbottom was recovered nine days later 360 miles away. When the Antarctic winter begins, the whales swim northward. They stay around South Africa, South America, Australia and New Zealand.

Northern Hemisphere whales have similar migration routes in winter and summer, but we don't know as much about them. They go from southern waters into the northern oceans. Some of the fin whales cross the equator. Those of the Southern Hemisphere may join those of the Northern Hemisphere.

Now radio and airplanes are used to give information about the movements of whale herds. Very recently an electric harpoon has been invented. It is fired from a gun and carries a charged wire which kills the animal instantly.

Until the invention of the first harpoon gun, very little was known about whales. Men knew how to kill them, but that was about all. No naturalist had made a study of their lives and habits. Museums had only a few skeletons. These were always from whales that had died and drifted ashore. Usually the bodies were blown up with gas, and the color had changed. Often many of the bones were lost. When whales were "cut in" beside a ship at sea, it was not possible to get photographs or measurements. No one was interested anyway.

At the shore stations all this was changed. The whales

were pulled entirely out of the water on a platform called the "slip." There they could be studied and photographed. Also a naturalist could go out on the little hunting vessels and learn the whale's habits.

About the time the first shore stations were built on Vancouver Island and in Alaska, I came to the American Museum of Natural History in New York City. The museum wanted whale skeletons and sent me to the Pacific coast stations to collect and study.

For eight years I lived only for whales. The work carried me twice around the world and from the Arctic to the tropic oceans. I spent many weeks on the vessels at sea. At that time no other naturalist had studied live whales. Therefore, almost all the things I saw and wrote about the habits of whales were facts people did not know. It was a great opportunity.

4.

Fin Whales and the Ugly Humpback

Fin whales, or rorquals, inhabit all the oceans of the world. They take their name from a boneless, sickle-shaped projection of skin and blubber on the lower back. It is only a foot or two in height and isn't a real fin. Probably it acts as a balancing organ. As years go on, it may get larger or disappear entirely.

Five kinds of fin whales make up the group. They are the humpback, sulphurbottom, finback, sei, and little piked whale. The last named is a small and rare species.

It is never taken by whalemen. Therefore, its habits are almost unknown. Perhaps Bryde's whale is another separate species. We are not quite sure.

Except for the humpback, all the fin whales have long, slender bodies. Their heads are flat and roughly triangular. The skulls are not arched as in the right whales because the baleen is short. The streamlined bodies make them fast swimmers. They feed on small shrimp about half an inch long. Their throats are small.

In all fin whales the blubber of the throat, breast and belly is divided into lengthwise folds like accordion pleating in a dress. The folds can spread apart widely. This makes the underside of the body very elastic. When the whale takes in air for a deep dive, the lungs can expand to their full extent. The right whale and bowhead do not have throat folds or dorsal (back) fins. They are quite unlike the fin whales in appearance.

The finback, sulphurbottom, sei and little piked whale are closely related and, in general, look alike. The humpback differs a good deal from the rest of the group, but it is one of the fin whales.

It is as unattractive as the other fin whales are beautiful. Its fifty-foot body is thick and stubby. The enormous side flippers, fifteen feet long, have unsightly knobs on the front edge. There are knobs on the chin and jaws and more knobs on the top of the head. Each one contains a short, stiff hair. The dorsal "fin" is a humplike projection which gives the animal its name.

The humpback is black as coal above. Patches and circles of pure white mark the under parts. Also the flukes and flippers are white below. Some individuals have a few white markings; others are entirely white on the breast and belly. I do not know of any completely white humpback.

The humpback has only about twenty-four rather wide folds on the under parts. In the other fin whales the folds are narrow and may number as many as eighty to one hundred.

Clusters of barnacles hang from the chin and throat of every humpback. They embed themselves in the flippers and flukes too. These are the same barnacles you see on wharf piles. They also attach themselves to ships' bottoms and to sea turtles. The "goose barnacle" has a five-inch muscular stalk, a hard shell and six pairs of feet. Such creatures must cause the whale much discomfort and certainly make the ugly humpback even more unattractive.

The humpback's mouth is enormous. On either side of

the upper jaw, the dull black baleen plates hang in two parallel rows. Each plate is roughly triangular. It is four inches wide at the base, pointed at the end and three feet long. The inner edges are frayed out into coarse, brownish bristles forming a thick mat. This strains out the little shrimp on which the whale feeds. The great flabby tongue weighs more than a thousand pounds and fills all the space in the mouth. Strangely enough it is bluish in color.

I examined my first humpback whale with great interest. The eyes were brown and lay just behind the corners of the mouth. They seemed very small for such a huge animal, only about twice the size of a cow's eyes. I don't think a whale's sight is very good, at least his sight above the surface. Probably under water he can see better, but he depends mostly on hearing.

If I had not known where to look, I would never have found the ear openings. They were tiny holes about three feet behind the eyes. Each opening was just large enough to admit the lead of my pencil. As I have explained, a whale doesn't need external ears because water transmits sound so very well.

I was curious to see for myself what had become of the humpback's hind legs. So I marked off a section

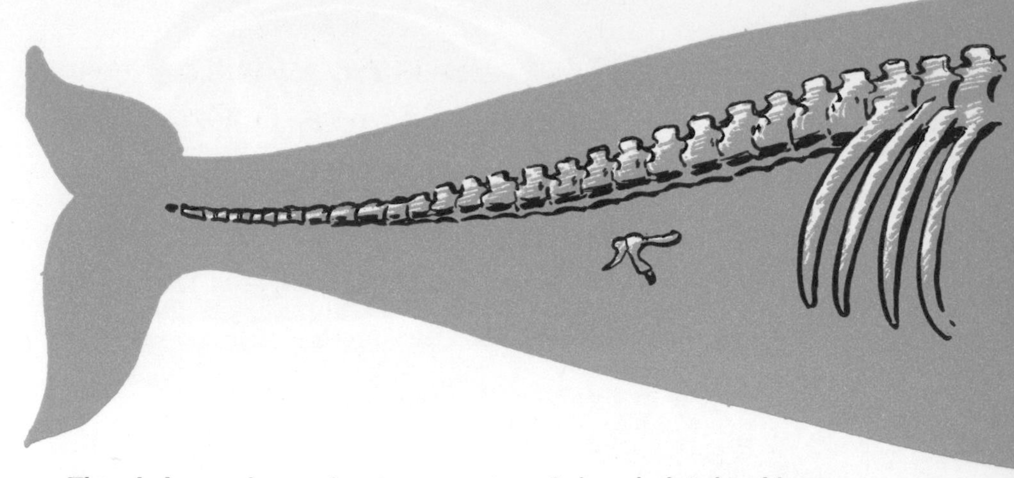

This skeleton shows the tiny remains of the whale's hind legs.

of the abdomen. I knew that was where the remains of the legs ought to be. One of the men sliced out the big chunk of flesh and blubber and pulled it off to one side. Later in the day I began cutting it up. Sure enough, deep in the flesh, the knife struck bone. Working around it, I took out three pieces. One was the remains of the pelvis. Attached to it was a four-inch bone, the femur, or upper leg bone. Only a little round chunk, about the size of a walnut, represented the tibia, or lower leg bone. On the other side was a matching set of bones. These are all that remain of the hind legs that the ancestors of whales used when they walked on land millions of years ago.

When I cut up the flippers, I found each had five

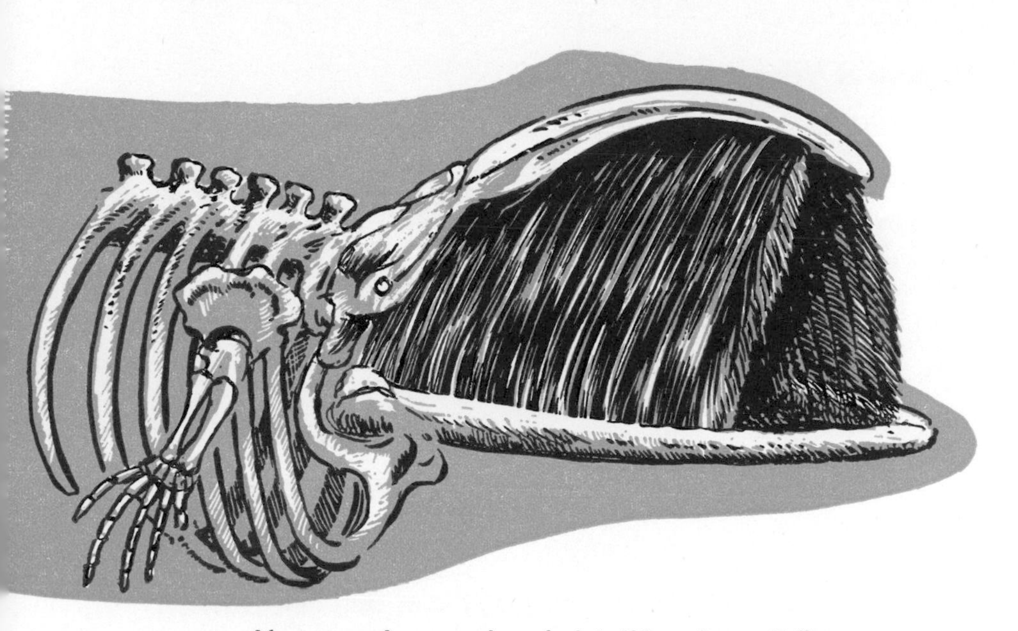

You can also see the whale's "five-finger" flippers.

fingers as in a human hand. Most of the bones and blood vessels of a land mammal's foreleg were there. The bones had simply been overlaid with tissue and blubber to make a paddle. They had not disappeared like the hind legs because they are useful for balancing and turning. They had been adapted for a new use.

When the humpback whale was "cut in" at the station, I was busy as a bee. First I took photographs. Then I wrote a description of the color and markings in my notebook. Twenty different measurements came next. I had to work fast, for the whale seemed to disappear like magic.

Men swarmed over the great body like flies. They made lengthwise cuts through the blubber from head to tail. Then they tore it off as you would peel an orange. Each strip is called a "blanket piece." That is a good name, for it is a warm blanket six inches thick.

The blubber is tough and fibrous and elastic. If a hook gives way, the blanket piece flies back with such force that it can flatten a man out like a dead fly.

In fifteen minutes one side of the whale was stripped of blubber. Then the "canting winch" turned it over. The other side was soon bare. Only the flesh and bones remained. The steam winch literally tore the carcass apart. The steaming red meat was cut into great chunks. The bones were sawed up. Blubber, flesh and bones were put into separate boiling vats. After the oil had been "tried out," the bones were crushed by machinery to make "bone meal," an excellent fertilizer. The flesh, dried and sifted, is also used for fertilizer.

A big whale contains several tons of blood. This was carefully drained from the slip into big vats. It was boiled and dried for fertilizer. Even the water in which the blubber had been tried out was converted into glue. The baleen was cleaned and dried. It is short and coarse and of no value in America. But the Japanese make many beautiful and useful things from it. Thus no part of the fifty-ton whale was wasted.

5.

Humpback Habits

I soon discovered that the humpback is the most interesting of all the large whales. He is so playful that you can never be sure what he will do. He may dash along the surface with his great mouth wide open, or stand on his head and "lobtail," or throw his fifty-ton body into the air. Let him alone, and he is quite harmless. But if attacked he will fight back savagely.

I learned a good deal about humpbacks in Alaska where I went after leaving Vancouver Island. The station was at Murderer's Cove, Tyee. We hunted mostly in Frederick Sound. Beautiful snow-capped mountains rose all about us, and the water was usually calm. I spent much time in the barrel at the masthead. From there I could see far down into the water. One time I watched a humpback swimming parallel with the ship. He was about twenty feet beneath the surface. When he wanted to turn, he would swing out his long flippers. But to go forward, he never moved them. Only his great tail waved up and down.

One day a playful humpback came up under the ship. I was thrown off my feet as the bow lifted, but I hung on to the camera and scrambled up. I just pointed it and pressed the button, knowing it would probably be a poor picture. But when I developed the plate, there was the huge body partly hidden by the vessel. It showed the whale just drawing in its breath with the blowholes wide open. Moreover, the photograph indicated something new. *The nostrils were raised far above the level of the head*. Doubtless this is to prevent a wave from slopping over into the nose. A very practical thing it is, too. But in a dead whale there is no indication that it can be done.

When a whale spouts, the sudden rush of air through

the pipelike blowholes makes a metallic, whistling sound. On a still day it can be heard for a mile or more. The early stories about whales say that they "roared" or "bellowed like a bull." That is quite untrue. Probably the noise of the spout was mistaken for a roar. By the sound of the spout you can distinguish between humpbacks, finbacks and sulphurbottoms.

The first whale I ever saw "breach," or leap out of the water, was a humpback in Alaska. We saw the whale's spout and ran up close before it sounded. It seemed certain that he would blow again. The ship lay quietly, rolling slowly in the swell. No one moved or spoke. Ten minutes dragged by. Then, without warning, a mountainous, dripping body heaved upward almost over our head. It seemed to hang for an instant in mid-air and fall back sideways. I stared at the thing, too surprised to use the camera. Even the nerves of the harpooner were shaken. He clung weakly to the gun without a move to shoot.

The whale dropped barely twenty feet away. If it had fallen in the other direction, it would have landed on us. The ship would have been crushed like an eggshell. Never since then have I known a whale to breach so close to a vessel.

Sometimes four or five humpbacks will leap out of the water together. Each seems to try to outdo the other. You can't imagine what a wonderful sight it is. Whalemen think this is done to free the body from barnacles. But I think it is merely play. Some other whales that have no barnacles do it also, but not so much as humpbacks.

Humpbacks perform another act almost as spectacular. This is called "lobtailing." The whale literally stands on its head. It begins to wave the gigantic flukes back and forth. The motion is slow and dignified at first, but gets faster and faster. Clouds of spray fill the air. The slaps on the water can be heard for a mile. Then the motion stops, and the whale sinks out of sight.

On a brilliant day in Alaska I watched a humpback feed. The water sparkled in the sun. From the barrel I could see for miles. Clouds of birds hovered in the air. They were eating little red shrimp about half an inch long that floated at the surface and gave the water a light pink color. The whale made a rush into the mass of shrimp. The great jaws opened taking in a quantity of water. As it closed its mouth, the soft flabby tongue forced streams of water out between the baleen plates. The mat of bristles on the inside of the baleen strained out the shrimp. Sometimes the whale rolled over on its side. Its fifteen-foot flipper stood straight up in the air. The ship kept getting closer and closer, but the Humpback paid no attention. It was too busy feeding. At last the Captain shot it. At the station I took four barrels of shrimp from the stomach of that one whale.

All baleen whales eat shrimp and other small crustaceans when they can get them. They eat small fish at times but very seldom. There are more fin whales in the Antarctic during the southern summer than anywhere else. That is because those waters have the most shrimp.

No one knows how deep a whale can dive. We can only guess. It is believed that a finback can descend to 1,150 feet and a sperm whale possibly reaches 3,000 feet, or more than half a mile. The water pressure is too great for humans to go down very far. For a person in a diving suit, five hundred feet is about the limit. A man has to rise very slowly so his body can accommodate itself to the change of pressure and get rid of nitrogen bubbles in his blood. If he doesn't, he gets the "bends" and may die. But whales go far down and come up within a few minutes. In some way Nature has adapted them to withstand water pressure that would crush a ship like an eggshell. Physiologists are just beginning to understand this remarkable adaptation to life in the sea.

Off the coast of Japan we harpooned a sulphurbottom whale. It dove straight down and took out a quarter of a mile of rope. After thirty-two minutes it came up less than a hundred yards away. I think it was down for the limit of the line. However, I couldn't prove it. Almost every whaleman will tell similar stories.

Humpback whales have a definite mating season like land mammals. In the Southern Hemisphere this is from August to November. Occasionally they do pair at other times of the year. The calf is carried eleven months. It is about fourteen feet long when born and weighs several tons. Of course it can grow so large because the water supports the mother's body and the weight of her baby. Besides the baby must be able to swim at birth. Like human babies young whales must be kept warm. So their blubber is much thicker than that of their parents.

Whales seldom have more than one baby at a time. Sometimes twins do occur but not often. The calf is nursed for five months. It is weaned when about twenty-five feet long.

For many years it was supposed that young whales

grew very slowly. They were compared to elephants, the largest land mammals. Elephants do grow slowly, but now we know that whales grow very rapidly. By the end of the first year a humpback calf will be more than twice as long as at birth. At the end of the second year, it is able to have young. Humpbacks usually give birth every two years.

It is impossible to know how long a whale lives. From the condition of the bones, you can tell whether

Four or five humpbacks will leap out of the water together.

it is young or old. But *how* old is another question. Humpbacks stop growing at about the age of ten. A harpoon that could be identified was taken from a humpback and showed that particular whale was eighteen years old. I would be surprised if any of the big whales live to be as much as fifty years old. But that is only my guess.

Like all whales and porpoises, humpbacks have great affection for their young. Neither a mother nor her baby will leave the other. If sharks or men attack, the mother will get between them and her offspring. There are many touching stories of this love. Captain Melsom told me that he killed a female humpback that had a good-sized baby. They made the dead whale fast to the bow of the ship, but even then the calf would not leave. It swam close beside the mother's body. When they reached the station and dropped the whale, the young one still remained. Not until its mother was pulled out of the water on the slip, did it swim away.

At sea I recorded how a humpback dives and spouts. The whale comes to the surface obliquely. At first only the top of the head shows as far as the blowholes. Instantly the spout is delivered. It makes a loud, metallic, whistling sound. The cloud of vapor shoots straight upward for about fifteen feet. It spreads out forming a low, bushy column which soon drifts away in a ball of mist. Even though there are two nostrils, the spout comes together as a single column. All the fin whales blow that way, but the right whales have a divided spout. The height and density of the spout depend upon how long the whale has been under water. If it has been down a long time, the breath will be hot and have much moisture in it. When a whale is lying at the surface blowing every few seconds, the spout can hardly be seen. Then there is little noise. As soon as the spout is delivered, the whale opens its nostrils widely and sucks in its breath.

When making a deep dive, a humpback will blow six or seven times before going down.This gets the lungs and the blood thoroughly filled with oxygen. If feeding at the surface, the whale blows only once or twice each time. Twenty-five minutes was the longest time I recorded a humpback to be under water. But they can certainly stay below much longer than that.

A humpback's "sounding" dive is really beautiful to watch. Right after the spout, the head is turned down and the body begins to revolve. It is arched in almost a half circle and lifted high out of the water.

As the revolution goes on, the flukes appear. They are first parallel to the surface. Then they are vertical to it, and the whale is literally standing on its head as it sinks from sight. The action is surprisingly smooth and graceful. When the whale takes a surface dive, its flukes are not drawn out and its back is not arched.

The distance covered when humpbacks are below the surface varies with conditions. When they are traveling, they may rise a mile or more from where they went down. If feeding, the animals may come up close to where they disappeared.

A smooth, circular patch of water always is present on the surface when a large whale dives. When it is rising, the same thing happens.

A humpback mother and baby stay close to each other.

Humpback Habits

All the fin whales migrate just like birds. Those of the Southern Hemisphere go from tropical waters to the Antarctic Sea, where they find great quantities of the shrimp that they like to eat. They go back to warmer waters when the winter sets in. There they mate and breed. Humpbacks of the Southern Hemisphere go up to the coast of Africa and Australia.

There are few barriers to restrict the migrations of water animals except temperature and food. Land mammals are barred by mountains, rivers, deserts and climate. Fin whales have no such handicaps. They can swim where they please and as far as they please. So we have fin whales of all kinds in the oceans of the Northern and Southern Hemispheres.

So many humpbacks have been killed that they may disappear altogether. That is because they are slow-moving whales that like to stay near the coast. When feeding and mating, they are easy to catch. Therefore, on any whaling grounds humpbacks are quickly killed off. When I first went to sea many years ago, there were more humpbacks than any other species. Now there are very few. The Japanese like the humpback meat better than any other whale so it brings a higher price and is greatly sought after.

6.

The Biggest Animal That Ever Lived

The sulphurbottom whale is the largest animal that ever lived on the earth or in its waters. Not even the greatest dinosaurs, that splashed along the shores of inland lakes more than 100 million years ago, could equal a sulphurbottom whale in length or weight. It dwarfs all other whales. One hundred eleven feet is the longest actually measured with a tape, but probably there have been bigger ones.

It is difficult to understand how enormous whales

really are. I couldn't realize it until I stood beside one. Then I looked at the gigantic beast in awe. It seemed like a mountain of flesh and blood.

In 1947-48 an American army officer, Lieutenant Colonel Waldon C. Winston, went with the Japanese whaling fleet to the Antarctic Ocean. He was there to see that the International Whaling Laws were being observed. On that cruise they weighed a sulphurbottom whale. They wanted a big one and, by good fortune, killed an eighty-nine-foot female. The female fin whales are always larger than the males. This lady was a real giant.

The animal was pulled on the slip in the stern of the "floating factory." As it lay on its side, the Japanese Chief Inspector clambered up the breast folds. It was like climbing a hill, for the whale was forty-three feet six inches in circumference. The flukes measured twenty feet from tip to tip. The flippers were nearly ten feet long. The lower jaw was twenty-two feet ten inches in length.

The whale was weighed in sections. The total weight was 300,707 pounds. That is more than 150 tons. It wasn't a fat whale either. The great flabby tongue weighed 6000 pounds and the liver 2000 pounds.

The heart tipped the scale at 950 pounds. With all the latest machinery and methods, it required eighty men, three hours and forty-five minutes to cut and weigh, part by part, the largest whale ever weighed.

The Japanese eat the meat and many of the other parts of whales. Therefore, each one is more valuable to them than to those people who only use the oil for refining and the meat and bones as fertilizer. This eighty-nine-foot whale yielded the Japanese company $27,900. The oil was valued at $9,900; the red meat, frozen and salted, at $18,000.

Besides being the largest of all whales, the sulphur-bottom is one of the most beautiful. Its long gray body is mottled with lighter patches. The head is plain gray and somewhat darker than the sides and back. A few pure white spots are usually present on the belly. The flippers are gray on the upper surface and white below. The flukes are gray above, but the underside is marked with fine light and dark gray lines from front to back.

Why the name sulphurbottom should have been given to the animal, I do not know. The Norwegians call it the blue whale, and that is a much better name. At a distance in the water, it does look as though its body had been washed with bluing. But the name sulphur-

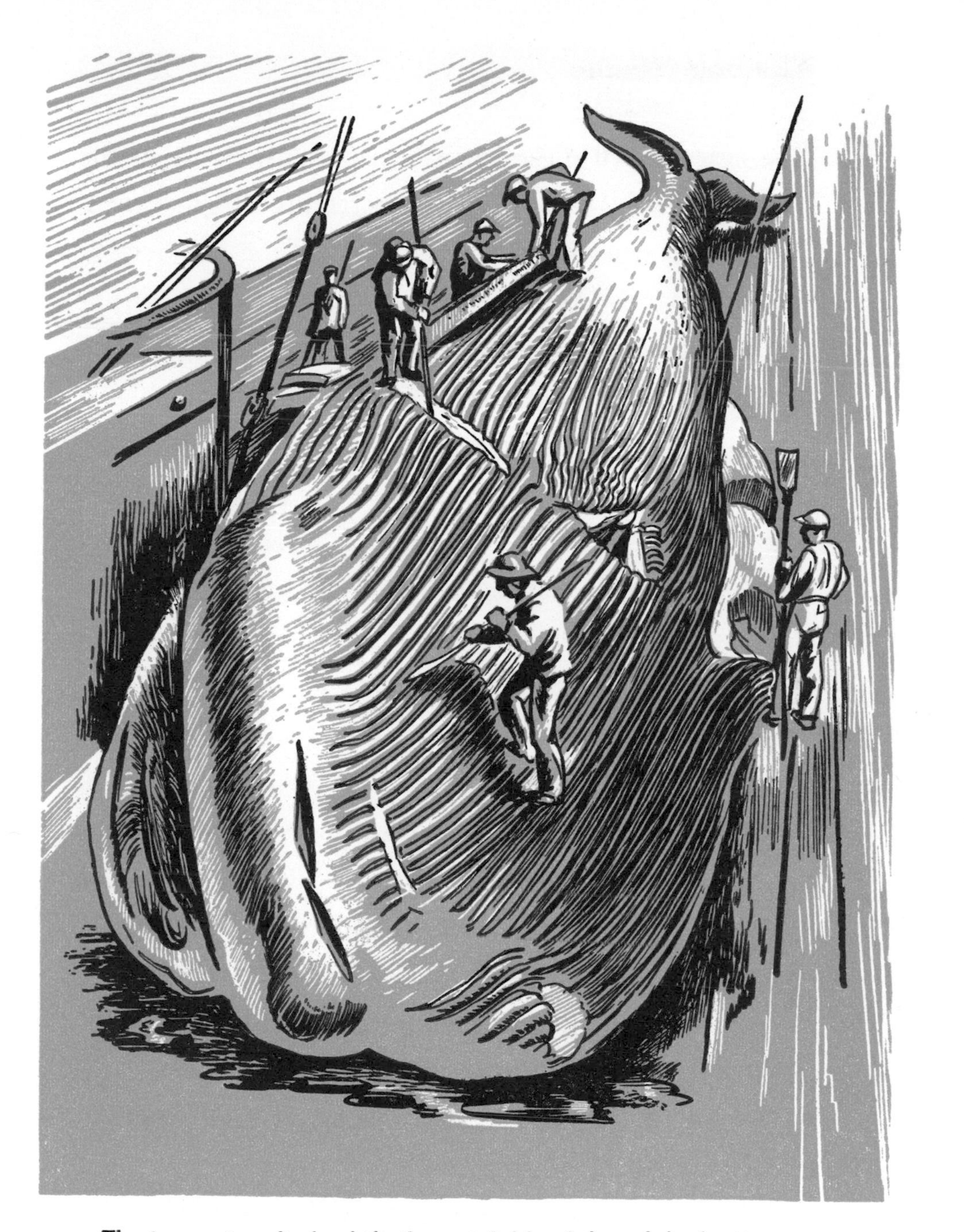

The inspector climbed the breast folds of the sulphurbottom.

bottom has become so firmly established that we must continue to call it that.

The sulphurbottom has brown eyes, not more than twice as large as those of a cow. Its chin bears thirty-two hairs. These are in a cluster just like chin whiskers. Fifteen or twenty may occur on top of the head, but some whales show none at all and are completely bald. The hairs are short and brittle, and each one grows from a little pit. Of course, they are the remains of the hairy covering whales once had when their ancestors lived on land.

The sulphurbottom seldom has barnacles like the humpback. The skin is clean, dry and soft. Sometimes the ends of the flippers are bitten off. They show teeth marks. This, I suppose, is the work of "killer" whales, a savage toothed species. It is possible that sharks may do it too.

The throat, breast and belly folds, or grooves, are more numerous in the sulphurbottom than in any other whale. They vary in number from eighty to a hundred. This "accordion pleating" allows expansion of the throat in feeding when the whale takes in a mouthful of water. Also the great lungs can be filled to their entire capacity.

I have a special love for the sulphurbottom because it started me on my whaling career. When I first came to the American Museum of Natural History, I helped build the life-size model of a sulphurbottom.

Our whale is seventy-six feet long and has been stared at by millions of visitors to the museum. She is still one of the most popular exhibits. While building that model, I read everything I could find about whales.

You can imagine how excited I was when I saw my first sulphurbottom. I *heard* the great whale long before I saw him. It was in Frederick Sound, Alaska. A thick fog had shut down. We couldn't see twenty feet. The ship "lay to" with engines stopped. All about us whales blew constantly. Many had followed a mass of floating shrimp. Humpbacks, finbacks and sulphurbottoms were feeding close together. I stood on the bridge of the ship with the Captain. Suddenly a hoarse bellow sounded. "That's a humpback," said Captain Grahame. Then came a higher pitched blast, quite different from the other. "A finback, certainly," he shouted. A little later a terrific whistling roar ripped through the fog. "That," said the Captain, "is a sulphurbottom and a big one."

He was right. When the fog lifted, an amazing picture met our eyes. On the smooth glassy surface, dozens of whales rolled and spouted. They were feeding ravenously. As their great mouths closed, streams of water spurted out from between the baleen plates. Three sulphurbottoms showed like giants among the finbacks and humpbacks. Captain Grahame examined them carefully with his binoculars. He pointed to a whale on the left less than a quarter of a mile away. "That one is a monster. He'll measure eighty feet at least. I want him."

The whales were so intent upon their breakfast that they paid not the slightest attention to the ship. With engines at half speed, the little vessel crept nearer. The beast looked like a gray mountain. Just before the gunner fired, I saw the cavernous mouth open and shut. Then the iron struck under the flipper. The biggest creature that ever lived on the earth or in its waters sank without a struggle!

At the station I examined that sulphurbottom with intense interest. I wanted to see if our work on the museum model had been well done. After studying the whale, I felt very happy. We could be really proud of the replica that hangs in the American Museum.

This whale was eighty-five feet four inches long.

What most impressed me was its tremendous size. Everything about it was awe-inspiring. Nature had really created a colossus.

Every whale hunter has stories to tell of the amazing strength and power of this giant. Some of them are almost unbelievable, but I have seen examples of it myself. Here is one story I know to be true. A sulphur-bottom was struck by a ship called the *Puma* off the coast of Newfoundland. At nine o'clock in the morning their iron hit right between the shoulders, but the bomb didn't explode. The barbs of the harpoon were only caught in the blubber. The whale was unhurt and could pull for all it was worth.

During the entire day the great animal towed the ship with the engines at half speed astern. Even against that force the vessel moved forward at seven miles an hour.

All through the night the whale dragged the ship. Also it had to carry the dead weight of two miles of heavy rope. At nine o'clock the next morning the whale seemed as lively as ever. By ten o'clock its strength began to fade. An hour later the gallant animal lay exhausted at the surface. It had put up a great fight for twenty-eight hours.

Many a sulphurbottom whale is eighty-five feet long.

One time my friend, Captain H. G. Melsom, struck a sulphurbottom off the coast of Siberia. It ran out nearly a mile of line. With engines going at full speed astern, it pulled the ship forward. At no time was the speed less than ten miles an hour.

In every case where a whale has towed a ship, the harpoon was embedded well forward. If struck near the tail end, the whale can't pull. The strain of the rope straightens out the body so the animal can hardly swim.

In the water sulphurbottoms continue to give the same impression of enormous size that they do when

That is about as long as a truck and three and a half cars.

pulled out on land. If they are swimming near any other whales, they make them look like pygmies. Their movements are ponderous and impressively dignified.

A sulphurbottom does not play like a humpback, which will throw himself out of the water or stand on his head. Neither does he roll over and over in the sheer joy of being a whale in the open ocean. He seems to take most seriously his distinction as the greatest animal that ever lived.

Like the other fin whales, sulphurbottoms rise to the surface obliquely. When the top of the head appears, the spout is delivered. The vapor shoots into the air like a geyser and with a tremendous whistling blast. It rises twenty to twenty-five feet in a slender but dense column. It is not rounded and bushy like a humpback's spout. Its height depends on how long the whale has been under water.

The sounding dive begins as soon as the whale spouts. Down goes the head, and the body begins to revolve, but not in as much of a half-circle as does the humpback. It is lifted higher and higher until the dorsal fin appears. Then it slowly sinks from sight. At no time are the flukes drawn out of the water. That would not quite fit the dignity of such a magnificent beast. The dive gives the impression of majestic force.

Like all other fin whales, the sulphurbottom feeds on the shrimplike crustacean, *Euphasia*. This little animal is known as "krill." The whale opens its cavernous mouth and takes in a great quantity of shrimp. Then it rolls on its side, closing the jaws. The water spurts out in streams from between the baleen plates. A flipper may show above the surface; also one lobe of the flukes. Sometimes the whale rolls from side to side as its huge mouth opens and shuts.

In the summer, sulphurbottoms of the Southern

The spout of the sulphurbottom (left) is slender but dense. That of the humpback (right) seems to be rounded and bushy.

Hemisphere go to the Antarctic water where there is more shrimp than any other place, and the whales feed heavily. They find little to eat during the winter in warmer waters. By summer they are thin whales.

Breeding habits of the sulphurbottoms are similar to those of humpbacks. The height of the pairing season is in June and July. The young are mostly born in April and May. The average size of calves at birth is twenty-three feet, but I measured one that was twenty-five feet long. Twins are rare. I have seen them only twice. A calf every two years is usual. The baby of the sulphurbottom grows very rapidly.

7.

The Fighting Finback

The finback is first cousin to the sulphurbottom. It is second in length, but the most beautiful of all whales. Its graceful, slender body is built like a racing yacht. No other whale can swim so fast for so great a distance. The largest I measured was eighty-one feet long, and that is close to the record. Most are about sixty-five feet in length. But it is by no means as heavy as a sulphurbottom because the finback is streamlined like a mackerel.

Its body is dark gray above and white below. The sides shade into a delicate light gray. The head is not the same color on both sides; usually there is more white on the right side than on the left. It is like that, too, on the lower jaw. The baleen is gray, striped with yellowish white. On the right side the front baleen is all yellowish white.

The narrow pointed head makes a splendid cutwater. The flukes are broad because the whale is a fast swimmer, but the flippers are rather small and lance-shaped. A sickle-like fin on the lower back gives the animal its name. The ventral folds, or grooves, average eighty-four, but there may be as many as 106.

Probably it is not often that the baleen whales will deliberately attack a ship. But finbacks have the reputation of being very dangerous.

On one of my first trips from the whaling station at Aikawa, Japan, we had a long fight with a finback. It came close to being the end for me in a horrible way. I was frightened nearly to death.

I had gone to sea with a gunner by the name of Johnson. At six o'clock the next morning the engines began to start and stop. That brought me out of a whaling dream. I knew we were chasing a whale and dressed hurriedly. I put on rubber boots and oilskins, for there was a drizzling rain. A heavy swell kept the ship dancing. From the bridge I saw a high, narrow spout shoot into the air. That showed it was a finback.

The gunner waved his hand. "He's a wild whale. I can't get a shot."

For a long time the animal seemed to be playing with us. He was neither feeding nor traveling. For no apparent reason he hung about. Sometimes he would turn under water and come up astern. Never were the dives very deep. He was about seventy feet long. Even so, his huge body was as graceful as a serpent.

At last he headed directly away from the ship. I thought he was gone for good. But instead the whale burst to the surface in a cloud of spray. At the roar of the gun I saw the harpoon strike between the shoulders. The giant figure rolled on its side and lay motionless. "*Shinda*," yelled the Japanese, meaning "Dead." But the finback was far from dead. Suddenly it righted itself. Then with a mighty smash of its flukes it dashed off.

Rope ran out so fast that the wooden brake on the winch smoked. One hundred, two hundred, three hundred fathoms were gone. At last the rush ended, and the whale sounded. The rope hung rigid as a bar of steel.

We waited fifteen minutes with no sign from below. Johnson was worried. "I don't want him to die down there," he said. "This line is weak. We might break it hauling him up. He is very far down."

After twenty minutes the rope began to rise. The whale appeared nearly half a mile away. The engines were stopped, but the vessel began to move—slowly at first, then faster and faster. We were dragged through the water at ten miles an hour.

"I got him in a bad place," Johnson said. "The bomb didn't explode. He's not hurt a bit. He can pull like everything."

And how he did pull! For half an hour the ship danced over the waves. Finally the whale sounded. After ten minutes he came up like a leaping salmon. His whole seventy-foot body shot into the air, then off on another rush. The men below called up that the line was almost gonc.

"How much is out already?" I asked.

"About three-quarters of a mile."

"How much have you got?"

"Don't know exactly. Two miles, I think. He may use it all. I never saw such a strong whale."

Finally the animal slowed. The engines were going

at half speed astern. Still the ship was dragged forward. Each time the whale sounded, the winch pulled in a little line. At eleven o'clock the finback began to weaken. Slowly the vessel crept up. The wind had died, but a big swell was running. The ship rolled and tossed like a wild thing. The line slacked as we dropped into the hollow of a swell. It tightened suddenly and snapped with a crack like a rifle shot. Johnson yelled for full speed ahead. He fired just as the whale disappeared. It was a long chance. We saw the harpoon shoot over the water in a wide semi-circle. It dropped on the whale's back. Came a muffled explosion, and the line slacked again. The bomb had blown out the spent harpoon! Our whale was free!

The ship rolled quietly in the swell. We waited to see what would happen next. The only sound was the groaning of a pump. At last Johnson pointed to the left. "There he is. A long way off."

All day the ship hung to the whale's track in the rain and fog. About four o'clock Johnson got another long shot. This time the harpoon held. The whale dashed off as though it had never been hit. But the rush soon ended. The finback's great strength was spent. It lay at the surface, blowing frequently. We could see the harpoon hanging over the back with only two prongs embedded in the blubber.

"I don't dare haul him in for another shot," Johnson said. "If he makes a dash, the iron will pull out. Mate, lower the pram. Lance him where he lies."

I had always wanted to see a lancing. "Will you let me pull an oar?" I asked.

"Sure, if you want to," he said with a grin.

The pram is a small boat. It can carry only three or four men. It is a handy little boat and can spin about like a top. The Japanese mate scrambled over the side. He carried a long, slender steel lance. A sailor was next to him, and I pulled the bow oar. The whale lay at the surface a quarter of a mile away. It was blowing every minute or two.

As we rowed out, dozens of black fins cut the water. Now and then came the flash of a white belly. Sharks, attracted by the whale's blood! Big fellows, they were, fifteen feet long. I loathe sharks. I don't quite know why, but they terrify me. I touched one with my oar. It rolled over showing its grinning, half-circle mouth and a row of wicked-looking teeth. It made me shudder.

We slipped up on the whale from behind. It lay high in the water. At least fifty feet of the body was above the surface. It was a beautiful animal, slender and sleek as a seal. I could have stretched out my hand and touched the smooth, gray skin. Never before had I been so close to a live whale. It looked awfully big—four or five times as long as our little boat. The water lapped quietly along its sides. Tiny streams, like wavelets on a sand beach, ran off its back. The first harpoon was half embedded between its shoulders. The broken rope trailed off behind. An ugly wound showed the work of the second harpoon.

Suddenly I did not want the whale to die. Before, it had been a wild beast to be chased and caught for food. Now it was something living and personal. Such a magnificent creature ought to swim away unhurt! The other men didn't feel that way, of course. To them it meant tons of meat and oil and money in their pockets.

The mate signaled to us to swing the boat about and back in. We sat with oars raised, ready to pull away. The mate stood up. He set his feet firmly and drove the long, thin blade downward. I gave a great heave and heard a sickening crack. My oar had broken short off! The boat pivoted against the whale's side. The body lifted like a gray mountain. I saw the flukes, twenty feet across, weighing more than a ton, waving just above my head. They seemed to hang in the air for endless seconds. Then, as in slow motion, they seemed to come down right on me. The tip missed my shoulder by a scant twelve inches. It caught the side of the pram, splintering it to bits.

I was in the water, oilskins and boots pulling me down. My head struck wood as I came up. It was what remained of the boat. The mate was swimming toward the pram. The Japanese sailor seemed to be stunned. He lay face up beside the wreckage. In a moment he

The whale lay at the surface blowing frequently.

The man slipped off the wreckage. I caught him by the hair and pulled him back.

A few minutes later the ship came up. Johnson fired a harpoon into the whale. Then he sent a boat for us. When we got to the station at Aikawa, we did what we could for the wounded man. The whole calf of his leg was torn away, and the shark's teeth had dug deep into the bone. The Japanese sailor lost his leg. We were lucky we had not all lost our lives.

The habits of finbacks and sulphurbottoms are very similar. What you say about one applies almost equally well to the other. The breeding time and habits, and the migrations, are nearly the same. The finback's spout is not quite so high or thick as that of a sulphurbottom because the whale isn't so big or so heavy. But it is difficult to distinguish between the two at a distance.

Today finbacks are the most abundant of the big whales. They are found in all the oceans of the world. If you are crossing either the Atlantic or Pacific and see a whale, you may safely say it is a finback. As with the sulphurbottom, the flukes are not brought out of the water when it dives. The animal simply lifts itself higher, arches its back and slowly sinks below the surface.

Finbacks and sulphurbottoms often travel fast under water for a long distance without rising to breathe. One time the whale ship *Rekksu Maru* was sixty miles off the coast of Japan. Trouble with engines caused the ship to stop. For about three hours I stood in the barrel at the masthead. There was not a sign of a whale. Suddenly four finbacks rose just in front of the ship. They began to feed and stayed for half an hour. Then they all sounded. They spouted again half a mile away and disappeared. Those whales could not have blown within five miles of the ship without being seen. The ocean was dead calm. In the brilliant sun the spouts glittered like clouds of silver dust. So they must have come from some distance under water.

Captain Grahame told me that in Frederick Sound a school of finbacks suddenly appeared in the same place every afternoon at four o'clock. It seemed as though they had been sleeping on the bottom. Actually, they had simply been traveling fast under water. For whales and porpoises sleep only at or near the surface.

Whales have a definite means of communication. Often six or eight will be widely separated. All of them will leave the surface together. After a time they come up at the same instant. This must have been at a signal.

The Navy developed apparatus to listen for submarines. With it their men can hear all sorts of underwater sounds. Some are like screeches or whistles. They believe these are made by whales. I am certain this is true because it has been proved to be so in the case of porpoises.

A good many ships have been injured or sunk by whales, but probably most of them were struck by accident. Just before a whale dies, it sometimes goes into what is called the "flurry." Then it dashes about wildly in every direction. The animal is quite blind in its rushes. If a vessel is near, it may be hit.

Just after I left Alaska, a wooden ship named the *Sorenson* was sunk by a finback. The whale had been struck by one harpoon and was lying quietly at the surface. The Captain thought it was dead and came in close. Suddenly going into its death flurry, the finback began charging about. The *Sorenson* tried to back away, but it was too late. Coming at terrific speed, the seventy-ton whale rammed the ship. Its great head tore the vessel almost apart. The men were just able to get into small boats before she sank.

8.

Charged by a Wild Sei Whale

For many years, the sei whale was supposed to be the young of either the sulphurbottom or finback. It is only forty to fifty-five feet long. At first glance it does look a good deal like a small finback. It has the same slender, graceful form and gray body.

Until shore stations were built, naturalists thought sei whales were very rare. They had been recorded only from the North Atlantic. When I went to Japan, I found the Japanese were killing a whale they called *Iwashi kujira* (sardine whale). For fifteen years they had been taking these whales by hundreds in the summer. The sardine whale proved to be the sei whale. Yet no scientist knew that sei whales even occurred in the Pacific. That shows how little was known about whales at that time. I sent two skeletons back to the American Museum in New York and wrote a book about sei whales.

The Norwegians call it sei whale because it arrives every year along the Finmark coast with the "seje," or black codfish. The Japanese name is not good. The whale's principal food is shrimp and small crustaceans. Only when it can't get those will it eat sardines or other small fish.

I had some interesting experiences hunting sei whales off the Japanese coast. They arrive near Aikawa, north Japan, in early June. During July and August they are more abundant than any other whale. Many were killed by a friend of mine, a young Norwegian, Captain Erik Andersson. He asked me to go out with him for a sei whale hunt. I was delighted because it is always exciting to see a new animal for the first time. Erik took his Japanese wife along. Her name was Chio-san. She had been at sea with him several times and loved the excitement. It is not often that women are welcome on a whale chaser, but the Japanese sailors liked Chio-san. She was pretty and brought them little presents so they were glad to have her aboard.

We slept on Erik's ship that night, for we were to sail at daylight. When I dressed next morning, sun streamed through the porthole. But the vessel was rolling in a long swell. At ten o'clock we sighted a school of sei whales. Slim and graceful, they looked to be about forty-five feet long. Their spouts sparkled like silver mist thrown into the air. Each spout resembled that of a finback, only not so high because the whale is smaller. The column went up only eight to twelve feet. I could see that the back (dorsal) fin was high and sickle-shaped —much higher than in a sulphurbottom or finback. That is what really distinguishes the whale in the water from all others.

Usually sei whales are easy hunting, but these were wild. They were blowing lazily at the surface and seemed half asleep. But when we neared them, they slid under water and rose again a mile or more away. I was much interested in the dive. It was very different from that of a sulphurbottom or finback. The sei whale came up very obliquely and delivered the spout instantly. Then the motion continued forward and downward. The body gradually sank lower and lower until it disappeared. The back was not arched like a finback, and there was no revolving motion. Little of the body showed above the surface. The flukes were never drawn out of the water.

For three hours we chased those aggravating whales. Erik was on the gun platform. I stood just behind him with my camera. Chio-san was curled up on a seat in a corner of the bridge.

At last Erik was disgusted. "Those whales are impossible," he said. "We'll leave them and see if we can find others."

The ship's bell rang four o'clock before we found another sei whale. The animal was feeding on shrimp and blowing frequently. He seldom stayed down long. The high dorsal fin cut the surface, first in one direction, then in another. Always it was the center of a screaming flock of sea birds that dipped into the waves and rose. The water flashed in thousands of crystal drops from their brown wings.

We came up at full speed. The whale had stopped

The whale was the center of a screaming flock of sea birds.

feeding and started to run directly away from us. As he rose to dive, I could see a mark behind the dorsal fin.

"That's an old harpoon scar," Erik said. "It's a bad sign. He may give us trouble after all."

The engines were at dead slow. Erik stood at the gun. He swung the weapon to and fro, his feet braced, ready to shoot. Every few seconds he called to the sailor in the barrel, "Do you see him?"

We waited six minutes. Then the man shouted, "He's coming. Fast. On the port bow."

In a second the water began to swirl and boil. We could see the shadowy form rise, check its upward rush and swim along parallel with the ship.

"No good. He won't come," Erik yelled. "A little more speed. More speed. He's leaving us. Half speed."

Never shall I forget the intense excitement of those few minutes. The huge gray ghost swam only six feet below the surface. But he was as well protected by the water as though it had been a shell of steel.

Erik shouted. "He won't come. No good. Yes, now. Now! I *shoot*."

In the camera mirror I saw the enormous gray head burst to the surface. The blowholes opened and sent out a column of vapor. Then the sleek body drew itself upward, water streaming from the dorsal fin. Came a deafening roar. Everything was blotted out in a great cloud of smoke. I pressed the button of the camera.

Before I could see, I heard the Japanese shout, "*Shinda!*" The next instant the smoke drifted away. There lay the whale on its side, motionless. Then it sank slowly. The rope hung straight down.

"He never knew what hit him." Erik grinned. In a few moments he gave the word to haul away. The engineer started the winch, but the line slacked and tightened again. It began to rise. The water dripped in little streamlets off its vibrating surface.

The whale blew a hundred yards ahead. There was a tinge of red in the spout. He lay quietly for a time. Then he turned and swam toward the vessel. He moved slowly at first, but faster every second. When almost opposite us, he suddenly went crazy. With a terrific slash of his flukes he dashed directly at the ship.

"Full speed astern," Andersson yelled, dancing about like a mad man. "He'll sink us! He'll sink us!"

The whale was coming at great speed. Buried in white foam, he lashed up and down with his tremendous flukes. In an instant he struck the ship. We had half swung about, and he hit a glancing blow. The little vessel trembled and heeled far over. The whale bumped along her side, running his nose squarely into the propeller. The whirling blades tore strips of blubber from the snout and jaws. He backed off astern. Then with the entire head projecting from the water, he swam parallel to the ship.

I had been thrown against the rail, but I hung on to my camera. As the whale plowed along, I pointed it and pressed the button. A moment later the great beast rolled on its side, thrust its flipper straight upward, and sank. It had been his "death flurry."

Sweat poured from my face and body. Erik was shouting orders in English, Norwegian and Japanese all at once. He realized, though I did not at the moment, what a narrow escape it was. If the fifty-ton whale coming at high speed had struck the ship squarely, it would have been the end. The head would have torn such a hole in her side that she would have sunk in seconds. The man at the wheel had saved us. By throwing the vessel about, he let her take only a glancing blow. By some miracle, too, the propeller blades were neither broken nor bent. It was simply the luck that had followed this ship ever since Captain Andersson took command.

The dead whale was hauled to the surface and inflated. Then the sailors made it fast to the bow, tail first. Erik, Chio-san and I went below for a cup of tea.

Fifteen minutes later we came on deck. I stood at the rail, looking at my first sei whale. Suddenly a dark shape glided under the ship's bow. I thought it was only imagination, but another followed and another. Soon from every side specter-like forms were darting swiftly and silently here and there. Sometimes a white belly flashed as one turned on its side.

These were giant sharks drawn by the blood trail!

Giant sharks were drawn by the blood trail.

They were like vultures gathering for a feast on some dying desert animal. I watched one gouge out a great cup-shaped chunk of blubber. Others came, each one accompanied by its little striped pilot fish, swimming just behind its fin. In ten minutes a score of white-eyed sea ghosts were tearing at the carcass.

Erik was furious. "They'll eat up my whale. We'll have nothing but the bones. Bring the small harpoons!"

Five or six sailors rigged hand harpoons. Erik thrust his iron into a shark's back. Even then the brute waited to snatch one more mouthful before it slid off the whale into the water. Two boat hooks were jabbed into its gills, and it was pulled on deck. I paced its length. Twelve feet long and not the largest of the school! The harpoons were too slow. Erik got his rifle. Firing into their heads, he killed thirteen sharks. The dead ones were torn in pieces by the others as they floated off astern.

I do not believe that the attack by that sei whale was intentional. It was simply dashing about in its death flurry and did not know what it was doing. Nevertheless, it would have been just as serious for us.

We know now that the sei whale is an abundant species and widely distributed. It is found on both sides of the Atlantic and Pacific Oceans and also in the waters of the Southern Hemisphere. Certainly it goes around Cape Horn. Probably some travel from the North to the South Atlantic and into the South Pacific Ocean. No other big whale seems to be so restless. Always it must be on the move. Sometimes sei whales swim long distances. Suddenly they appear in great numbers where they were never known before.

The sei whales of the Southern Hemisphere spend the winter around South Africa. In the summer they go only as far south as the island of South Georgia, in the South Atlantic Ocean. Seldom are sei whales found near the edge of the ice, for they are temperate water whales and don't like too much cold. In the Pacific, sei whales winter in the warm waters and go north along the coast of Japan in June. Their annual migrations are quite regular in all oceans.

Most hunters won't kill sei whales if they can get the bigger kinds. They are so small and slender that the yield of oil and fertilizer is hardly worth the trouble. But in Japan the flesh is rated as good. So the Japanese hunt them for food all summer when sulphurbottoms and finbacks have gone farther north.

The sei is a beautiful whale. Its back is dark bluish-gray, shading gradually into light bluish-gray on the sides. The body is marked with wavy gray lines. The throat and breast are white but the bottoms of the folds, or furrows, are usually pinkish. A dark gray band runs across the belly. All over the body are oval-shaped white scars. The dorsal fin is much higher than in any of the other fin whales.

The throat and breast folds, or grooves, number thirty-two to sixty-two. The baleen is fine in texture and deep blue-black. Some plates are striped with white or gray. Twelve hairs are usually present on each side of the lower jaw in vertical rows.

The habits of the sei whale are much like those of the other fin whales. Briefly the story is this. In the Southern Hemisphere the mating months are from May to August. This is in the warm waters about South Africa. These whales have calves every two years. The baby is carried for twelve months and is fourteen feet long at birth. It is nursed for five months and is about twenty-seven feet long when weaned. The oldest sei whale in which the age could be estimated was fifteen years old. About ten percent more males are born than females. Thus, you see, this whole group of fin whales doesn't vary much in its life history.

For a short dash, the sei can swim faster than any other big whale. Probably it is able to reach thirty miles an hour. But it soon tires. As whales go, it is not very strong because it isn't very big. A sei can't tow a ship for hours as a sulphurbottom or finback does. The sei whale is like the cheetah, or hunting leopard. For a hundred yards or so the cheetah can reach seventy miles an hour. But after its first dash thc speed ends.

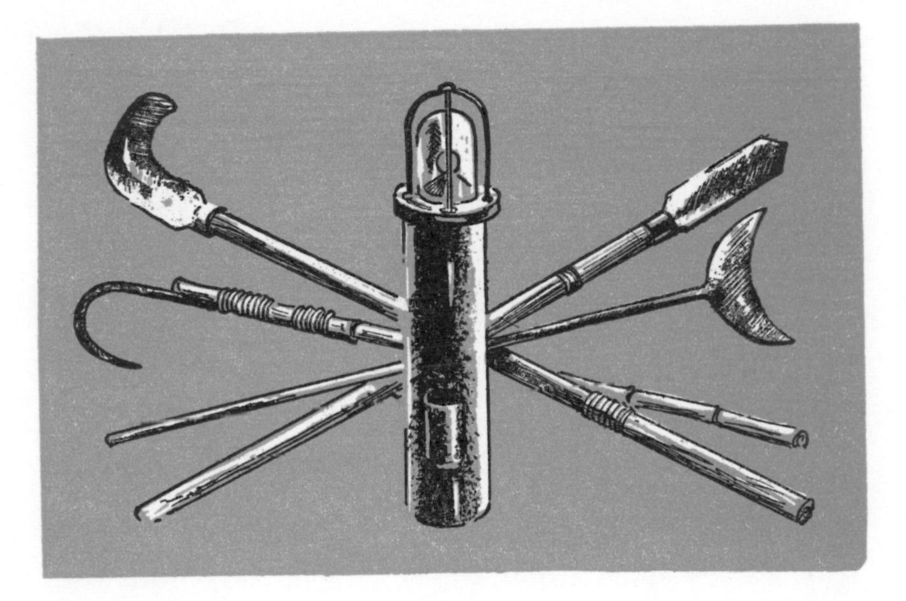

These tools were used to "cut in" a whale. The beacon light (center) was used to mark killed whales.

9.

Right Whale and Bowhead

The right whales represent a group that is quite unlike the fin whales. Instead of being long and slender like fish, the right whales are short and stubby. Their bodies are thick and ponderous with enormous heads. Somehow they make me think of an elephant. The side flippers of the fin whales, except the humpback, are small and lance-shaped. Right whale flippers look like short, broad paddles. The fin whale's head is flat and wide and the baleen only three or four feet long. A right whale's head is narrow and arched like a bow. The baleen of the Greenland right whale measures ten to fourteen feet. The fin whales all have throat and belly folds, or grooves. The right whales have none. They do not need to increase the throat capacity in that way because their heads are so large. Neither do they dive deeply as do the fin whales. The right whales do not have a dorsal fin.

Until the early nineteen hundreds, right whales used to be killed off the coast of Long Island, New York. A boat was kept ready in the villages to put out whenever a whale was sighted. While James L. Clark and I were building the sulphurbottom model, a right whale was taken at Amagansett, Long Island. The Museum Director, Dr. Bumpus, told Jimmy and me to go out there in a hurry. "Get the whole thing," he said. "Photographs, measurements, baleen and skeleton—every bone." Afterward we learned that he did not think we could do it because a whale on the beach is much harder to handle than at a shore station where a steam winch is used. On the beach the bones sink into the sand and are difficult to recover.

At Amagansett the business of buying the whale was quickly done. The baleen alone cost $3200 although it would be almost worthless today. The skeleton was given to us, but we had to get it ourselves.

The carcass was beached just at the edge of low tide. The fishermen stripped off the blubber and went away. The bones lay in some sixty tons of flesh. To get them out was a real problem. The fishermen did not want to work because of the cold. The thermometer stood at twenty degrees above zero.

Finally we did persuade half a dozen to help us. They hacked away at the carcass with big knives. With ropes and hooks a horse dragged off pieces of meat to the factory. At last the great head was separated. Three horses pulled it up the beach with the ribs of the upper side. Then the worst happened. A storm blew up. We saw it coming and anchored our whale as best we could.

For three days the shore was a smother of white surf. Anxiously we waited. Only half the skeleton was secure. That would be almost worthless if the rest were lost. The fourth day was calm and bright but very cold. Twelve degrees above zero at noon! On the beach there was not a sign of a skeleton. But our anchor ropes extended down into the sand. Shoveling exposed the bones. It was terribly difficult to separate the huge backbone. And the ribs of the lower side were deeply buried. As soon as we dug out a shovelful of sand, water filled the hole. We had to feel blindly with small knives. Our arms were always in freezing water.

Jimmy and I worked alone for three days. Every few minutes we warmed our hands over a driftwood fire. It seemed hopeless. But the museum director had said, "Get all the bones." We couldn't give up. At last some of the fishermen decided to help. I think it was shame that brought them around rather than the high wages we offered. Anyway half a dozen came, and we began to make real progress.

At the end of a week a huge pile of bones lay well up on the beach. We checked them off one by one on a drawing of a right whale skeleton. They were all there except the rudimentary leg bones. The director had said to watch for them particularly. Search as we would, Jimmy and I could not find those wretched bones. They were all that prevented us from doing a perfect job. Suddenly I had an idea. They might be in the flesh that the fishermen pulled off when they stripped the blubber. We got to the try works in a hurry. Some blubber had just been thrown into a huge iron pot. With a long-handled wire net I fished about. In two minutes I scooped out the bones. Now we could go back to New York with a clean bill of bones!

The Amagansett whale had with her a calf thirty-eight feet long. When its mother was killed, it left and swam aimlessly along the shore. Off the village of Wainscott other fishermen killed it. I purchased that skeleton also.

The director let me describe the Amagansett whale in a scientific paper. She measured fifty-four feet and was the largest right whale ever scientifically recorded. Moreover, the skeleton was the only complete one in any museum of the world. And that was after 1000 years of hunting the right whale!

The whale did not look like any creature I had ever seen before. I don't think I can give you a real impression of it. I'll try, but you must look at a picture to understand the animal. The body was coal black with only a few white splashes on the belly. That is the usual color, but some individuals have much white below. It varies a good deal.

The most amazing thing about the beast was the great, bowed head. The front part formed a narrow arch, and from it hung 250 black baleen plates. These were nearly seven feet long with ten-inch bristles. They were quite different from the three- or four-foot plates of the fin whales. The baleen is very elastic and folds

As the boat passed over the neck, the harpooner thrust a hand-bomb iron into the body.

back on either side of the tongue when the mouth is closed. The lower lips were nearly six feet in height. These fitted to the sides of the arched upper jaw.

On the snout our right whale had a rough area called the "bonnet." This has been the source of much speculation. It is covered with small crustaceans known as "whale lice." Other rough spots line the head from the bonnet to the blowholes. Some occur on the lower jaw too. They are like big corns. Just why the right whales have them, we can not say. But the fact remains that every right whale, male or female, wears a bonnet on its head. I counted 150 white hairs on the snout. About the same number formed chin whiskers. No fin whale has so much hair.

Right whales like temperate water. They do not go into the ice either in the Arctic or Antarctic. Neither can they endure very warm water. For that reason those in the Southern Hemisphere do not cross the equator into the northern oceans. Since they apparently never mingle, naturalists thought they represented different species. Whether or not that is true remains to be seen.

Right whales used to occur in great numbers in the waters of both hemispheres. Much hunting was done in the South Atlantic, Indian and South Pacific oceans. It was not confined to coastal waters.

Although right whales have been known for so many centuries, naturalists have studied their habits very little. They eat the little shrimp and various crustaceans. Apparently the female has a calf every two years and nurses it for twelve months. In this respect it is like most other large whales.

The right whale and bowhead are the only species in which the spout is divided. It is V-shaped and directed forward. One observer says about a right whale: "It kept blowing with a loud tinny noise. It was as though it was blowing at the end of a long drain pipe."

Sometimes the right whale is very playful. Again and again it will spring nearly clear of the water. Or it will roll on its side, whacking the water with one flipper. This playful nature of the right whale is very much like the play of humpbacks.

Right whales are easy to kill, and the females and calves were hunted without mercy on their breeding grounds. As a result the whales are very scarce now. In some waters they are protected by law. Nevertheless, it will be many years before they reach anything like their former numbers.

The bowhead is a larger edition of the North Atlantic

right whale. Its formal name is the Greenland right whale, but it is usually called bowhead. That is a good description, for the head is enormous and arched like a drawn bow. It is more than one-third the length of the whale. Unlike the right whale the bowhead does not wear a bonnet. The greatest length is sixty-five feet. The color is black with a little white about the throat and lips.

In some specimens the baleen reaches fourteen feet and is very fine and elastic. It used to sell for four or five dollars a pound. A large whale would have 3000 pounds of baleen. So that alone was worth twelve to fifteen thousand dollars. In addition there was the oil. If a ship took two or three whales in a season, it had a profitable voyage.

The baleen was used in corsets, dress-stays and whips. It was also used in many other articles where strength, lightness and elasticity were required. But after a while substitutes were invented. These were as good as whalebone and cheaper. So it was no longer profitable to outfit expensive vessels, and bowhead whaling ceased.

The bowhead is a true ice whale. It lives only in the Arctic Ocean, near Greenland, in Hudson's Bay and the Bering and Okhotsk seas. There are not many bowheads

The bowhead, or Greenland right whale, is a true ice whale.

left. Bering Sea probably has more than any other waters. When the ice breaks in the spring, the whales follow the coast eastward. They go past Point Barrow, Alaska, and as far east as Bank's Land. In the fall they return westward toward the Siberian coast.

The bowhead feeds on small crustaceans called "brit." These are strained out by the mat of baleen bristles as in other whales. Bowheads are very timid and easily frightened. Their hearing is so keen that ships could not use steam when hunting them. The noise of the propellers could be heard at a long distance and would send the whales off in a hurry. No bowhead would ever be seen. So the vessels would tie up to an ice floe and watch for whales from the masthead.

When a whale was seen, two or three small boats were lowered. The blowholes of the bowheads are on the top of a high hump on the head. Just behind them is a deep hollow over the "neck." When the whale lies at the surface, only the blowholes and back show. The attacking boat used no oars. It sailed up from behind and tried to cross directly over the neck. As it passed, the harpooner thrust the iron of a hand bomb into the body. When the bomb exploded, the animal was sometimes killed instantly. If the whale didn't die at once, there was trouble. It might dive under an ice floe. If the boat did not have enough rope, the line must be cut. Otherwise the boat would be wrecked. That was the way the American whalers who went to the Arctic killed the bowhead.

But the Eskimos did it differently. To them, getting a bowhead might mean food or starvation. As far back as tradition goes, the Eskimos of northern Alaska have been mighty hunters and whalemen. At the largest villages, near every cape and headland, the passing of the long winter's night meant preparations for the great "devil dance." This was the beginning of the spring whale hunt.

About April first the Eskimos built a road across the ice to the water. On this they could haul their skin boats and sleds. As weapons they had flint-headed harpoons and a few feet of walrus-hide line. To this were tied sealskin bladders.

If a bowhead was sighted, all the boats took up positions in nooks of the ice floe. When the whale came near, a ceremony was enacted. The head man of the village sang the "death song" handed down from some famous whale-killing ancestor. Then the chief thrust his harpoon into the whale. It did little except frighten the animal nearly to death.

As the bowhead passed the next canoe, the same performance was repeated. Only from then on there wasn't any song. Finally so many skin floats were attached to the whale that it couldn't dive. Then the natives killed it with their lances. The meat, blubber and bone were divided equally and sent ashore on sleds.

Today Eskimos use the white man's methods. They have harpoons, guns and bombs. They still take bowheads every summer for their meat. But the New England whalemen come no more. Bowhead hunting is only a memory to a few men who were part of the great days of deep-sea whaling.

Pygmy Right Whale

The pygmy right whale belongs to a separate family of its own and is the pygmy of the group.

In general it looks like a right whale, but everything about it is on a reduced scale. The greatest length is only twenty feet. It has a small dorsal fin but no throat furrows. The baleen is slender and white. In color the whale is black with a line of white along the belly. There are many peculiar characteristics about the skeleton such as the very wide and flat ribs.

The pygmy right whale has been found only near New Zealand. It is very rare, and nothing is known of its habits.

10.

Rediscovering an "Extinct" Whale

California gray whales have an interesting history. More than a hundred years ago, they used to appear along the coasts of British Columbia, Washington, Oregon and California. Their migrations were as regular as the seasons. In December they hurried southward to give birth to their young in the warm waters of the Mexican lagoons. In May they returned to the cold Bering Sea. They came close inshore, nosing about in the brown seaweed, or kelp, fields. Sometimes they wallowed in the surf like great seals.

The coastal Siwash Indians awaited their coming with eagerness. To them it meant a time of *potlatch* or feasting. In their frail dugouts, they hung about the floating kelp and harpooned the animals. A forty-foot whale gave them a lot of meat. But the whales were not stupid. After a while they got tired of being continually hunted. No longer would they come inshore but kept far out to sea. Soon they were heard of no longer.

But in 1854 Captain Charles Scammon, a New England whaleman, rediscovered them. Scammon was a pretty clever skipper. He used to sail around Cape Horn in the brig, *Boston*, with other New Bedford whalers. Some of the ships might stay out for two or three years before they got a full cargo. But not Scammon! After a few months he always returned home loaded with oil. The other whalers couldn't figure how he did it, and Scammon wouldn't tell. Neither would his crew, for they got a share of the big profits.

What happened was this. One winter day Scammon's boats chased several whales into the breakers along the shore of southern California. Surf piled in white lines over nasty-looking sand bars. Here the animals suddenly vanished. They just dived and disappeared like ghost whales. Scammon wasn't superstitious. He knew there must be an answer somewhere!

In a small boat he explored the edge of the shore. At last he discovered a narrow channel of deep water. It ran through the surf and gave entrance to a big lagoon that cut far into the desert. Whales, thousands of them, played about in this secluded bay. Many were females with newly-born calves. Never had a whaleman seen anything like it!

Scammon returned to his ship seething with excitement. Foot by foot he worked the *Boston* through the narrow passage into this whaler's paradise. There he could send out the small boats and watch his men kill whales. It was as easy as catching trout in a hatchery.

But the whales didn't submit tamely to being slaughtered. Often they turned furiously on the boats, smashing them to bits. Many sailors came in with broken bones. Some never returned. It was a continual battle of men against whales. The crew members were willing to take the risk because they were making so much money. They called the gray whale "devilfish" because it fought for its young so savagely.

For several years Scammon kept the secret of this hidden lagoon. One season the other whalemen set a watch on him. But at night he managed to slip into the lagoon unseen. His ship disappeared just as the whales had disappeared. The men in the vessels spying on him were completely mystified. At last they found him by smell. A New Bedford ship was sailing north of Cedros Island. There was an offshore wind. The Captain sniffed a familiar odor. "That's burning blubber sure as my name's Josh Hall! Bring her about. Slide up to those breakers," he said.

The Captain was right. A lookout in the barrel saw the masts of Scammon's ship showing above the sand dune at the entrance to the bay. Josh Hall soon found the narrow channel, and the secret was out. That spelled the doom of the gray whales. The news flashed through the whaling world like the discovery of gold in California in 1849. The next year forty or fifty ships went out for gray whales. They hunted them in every lagoon up and down the coast where the great creatures came to give birth to their young. Cows and calves and bulls were slaughtered without mercy. After a few seasons there seemed to be no more devilfish. This was about 1858. So far as scientists knew the species had been exterminated. The gray whale, or devilfish, was as dead as the great auk or the dodo bird. All that remained was a short account written by Scammon in a book on water mammals and a few bones in museums.

When I was in Japan in 1910, I learned of a whale called the *Koku kujira* (devil whale). It appeared along the east coast of Korea in the winter, traveling southward close inshore. Its description and habits sounded like Scammon's description of the lost California gray whale. But I could hardly believe it. The gray whale was extinct! I might just as well think about rediscovering a dinosaur!

Nevertheless, the thought remained in my mind. I determined to go to Korea and find out what the "devil whale" might be. If it was not the California gray whale, it must be a new species. Either prospect was exciting enough. One doesn't discover a new kind of big whale very often. So on a bitter cold night in January, 1912, I went aboard a little meat ship in Japan. We were bound for the whaling station at Ulsan, Korea, forty miles north of Pusan. We had a bad trip across the Sea of Japan. Tremendous waves washed the deck, soaking us to the skin. Five of us were crowded into a cabin only big enough for two. Everyone was seasick. I was miserable. Before we arrived, I wished I'd never heard of a whale.

The station was like those in Japan. I was given a room in the stationmaster's house and went to bed exhausted. But it was for only a short time. Just after midnight a terrific blast of whistles shook the house. A whale had arrived. This was my big chance. Either I was to discover a new species or one that had been lost to science for half a century. I forgot that I was tired. Pulling on hip boots and a heavy coat, I ran to the wharf. Flares already threw weird shadows over the bay. Out of the blackness a ghost ship slid into view. She was clothed in shining ice from bow to stern. The black flukes of a whale swung at her bow.

The shape of the tail was different from any other whale I knew. It was covered with white barnacle scars. There was no dorsal fin and the ridge of the back was scalloped. Then the winch hoisted up the body, and the head appeared. That did it! I knew it was the lost California gray whale! I was much happier than if it had been a new species. There is something romantic about discovering a supposedly extinct animal. It is like finding a living dinosaur or a pirate's treasure.

The *Rex Maru* brought two more whales next morning. There was plenty of time to measure and photograph the animals. Before the season ended, I examined

One man stood at the harpoon gun.

thirty-five. Moreover, I had two hundred photographs —the first ever taken of gray whales. Two complete skeletons were shipped to America. One went to the American Museum of Natural History in New York, the other to the Smithsonian Institution in Washington.

The gray whale is quite different from the fin and right whales and combines characteristics of both groups. Its habits are just as unusual and interesting. To study them I often went to sea with my friend Captain Melsom on his ship *Maine*. He was the man who first showed the Japanese how to take gray whales.

Always the weather was rough. The wind never ceased to blow on those bitter cold days. Sometimes as we stood at the gun, we were covered with ice. Our oilskins were stiff. If we did not shift our feet often, we might be frozen to the deck. But I did learn much about gray whales.

They begin to appear at Ulsan about the end of November on their southward migration. Females carrying young come first. A little later both males and females are seen. From the 7th to the 25th of January, only males are present. All the females have passed, and the migration is completed. As the babies must be born soon after passing Ulsan, their nursery must be in the bays of South Korea. When going south, the whales hurry straight ahead. They are never accompanied by small calves. But on the return trip north young are following their mothers.

A comparison of my observations with those of Scammon are interesting. The pattern of the migration of both herds is the same. The dates are alike. Also their breeding grounds in the bays of Korea and Lower California are in very nearly the same latitude.

During the summer the Korean gray whales live in the Sea of the Okhotsk. The California herd are in the Bering Sea and farther north. Perhaps they mingle and interbreed, but no one knows.

Their young are from twelve to seventeen feet long

when born. During a period of less than three months, the whale grows nine or ten feet; it grows eighteen feet in a year.

When swimming along the shore, the animals remain under water only seven or eight minutes. They blow three times after coming up. The "sounding" dive is much like that of a humpback. As soon as the spout is delivered, the body begins to revolve. Finally the flukes are drawn out of the water and sink under slowly. But they do not always "fluke out." During the surface dives only a small part of the back is shown and the tail never.

I could not find out what the gray whales eat. Neither could Scammon. The thirty-five that I examined had only dark green water in their stomachs. It would appear that on the southern migration they do not feed at all. This is not unusual for water mammals. Probably the gray whales go without food until they return to the north.

The devilfish are afraid of "killer" whales, which are the largest of the porpoise family. They are twenty to thirty feet long and have a mouth full of great curved teeth. Their tremendous strength and ferocity make them the terrors of the sea. They will attack anything that swims. Gray whales have a miserable life when killers are about. These sea wolves particularly like the whale's tongue. While hunting with Captain Melsom, I saw them attack a devilfish.

We were following a whale only a mile offshore. He was wild. He kept blowing once or twice and then sounding. We could never get close enough for a shot. Suddenly in the distance we saw a cloud of spray and great six-foot dorsal fins. A pack of killers were coming. They ploughed through the water and leaped into the air. On they came, making straight for our whale. As the beast rose to blow, he saw or heard the killers. His whole body seemed paralyzed with fright. He never tried to dive or get away. Instead he turned on his back and lay motionless with flippers outstretched. He just awaited his fate. The killers went at him like tigers. One pushed its nose against the gray whale's lips and forced its head into the mouth. I could see it tearing out great chunks of the soft tongue. Others leaped into the air, falling with a terrific thud on the whale's belly. The gray whale made no effort to save itself. The ship moved up, and Melsom fired a harpoon into its breast. As the bomb exploded, the whale sank from sight. I was glad its misery had ended.

The killers continued circling about the vessel. They were furiously angry. The sailors fastened the devilfish to the ship's bow. Then one of the killers attacked the carcass. It still tried to get at the tongue. Captain Melsom fired two bullets from his rifle into its head. The killer lashed out with its tail, smashing the ship's rail. Then it dashed off to join the others.

Of the thirty-five gray whales I examined, seven had the tongues more or less eaten. In one it was entirely gone. Sometimes a school of seven or eight whales will be attacked. They may all become paralyzed with fright and turn on their backs. At other times they will head for shore and get behind rocks where the killers won't follow them. The killers are not afraid of ships and do not leave when vessels arrive.

Captain Melsom told me that a school of gray whales can be stampeded like cattle. Sometimes three or four ships will be hunting the same herd. The vessels draw together. The ships go full speed at the whales while the sailors beat tin pans. They drop chains on the deck and make as much noise as possible. The whales dive at once. As soon as they rise to spout, the ships rush at them again. The whales go down but do not stay under long. The dives become shorter and shorter. Finally

A pack of killers made straight for our whale.

One tore out great chunks of the whale's tongue.

the whales are ploughing along at the surface.

The devilfish are "scared up." They become so terrified that they do not even remember how to escape. It is not always possible to stampede a herd. Often the animals will disappear at the first sound and swim away under water. If killers are about, it is easy to produce a stampede.

Captain Melsom said gray whales are not always so stupid. One day he was hunting an old bull in a perfectly smooth sea. The animal had been down for fifteen minutes. Suddenly a slight sound was heard near the ship. A cloud of vapor floated up from a small patch of ripples. The whale had just exposed its blowholes, spouted and refilled its lungs. Then it sank. It was almost noiseless. The gunners say this is not unusual when a single whale is being hunted.

The following winter I studied the bones and wrote a book about the gray whale. The job was fascinating, for no other whale is like the devilfish. It stands between the right and fin whales. The body is not as slender as that of a finback nor as thick as a right whale. The skull is neither as flat as in the former nor as arched as in the latter. The flippers are midway between the two groups in shape. There are only two to four short furrows on the throat and no dorsal fin. The back ridge of the body is scalloped. The flukes are convex on the outer edge instead of being concave as in the fin whales.

Both the right and fin whales came from the same stock originally. But millions of years ago each group began to have different habits. So Nature changed their bodies to fit them for the kind of life they wanted to live. The right whales developed the enormous arched head, very long baleen and thick body. The fin whales went along the lines of speed with a shorter, flat head and streamlined body. Our gray whale combines characteristics of both groups. It is not closely related to any of the other living whales and has been put in a separate family of its own. It is what is called a "primitive species." The skeleton bears this out. For instance, the bones of the rudimentary hind limbs and pelvis are much bigger than in any other species. Many characteristics show its relationship to an ancient whale called *Plesiocetus*, that lived in the Pliocene Period seven or eight million years ago. One might say that the gray whale is a "living fossil."

At one time, long before the dawn of history, it existed in the Atlantic Ocean. Now it is to be found only in the Pacific. Why it left the Atlantic and how it got to the Pacific, is anybody's guess.

The gray whale isn't a beautiful animal. The name does not fit it very well. The body is black or very dark slate and has only the suggestion of a gray "bloom." Its snout, lips and jaws are thickly marked with white spots and flecks. The sides, breast and belly have many irregular grayish patches. Both flippers and flukes are black all over, but with scattered white spots and circles. Probably these are the scars left by barnacles.

As in all baleen whales the females are larger than the males. They average about forty-one feet and the males thirty-nine feet long. Any specimens longer than forty-five feet are very rare.

The gray whale has from two to four short furrows on the throat. They do not extend back on the breast or belly as in the fin whales. This is because the devil-fish is a shallow-water species. Because of its feeding habits it takes in a comparatively small quantity of water at one time. Thus considerable expansion in the throat is unnecessary.

The tongue is narrow, thick and solid. It resembles that of a right whale. It is not at all like the soft, shapeless tongue of a fin whale.

The baleen, too, is very different. It is heavy and thick and has few plates. There are only 138 to 174 on each side instead of 250 or more. The bristles are round and very coarse.

The flippers and flukes are individual in shape, and the scalloped line of the lower back ends in a rounded hump.

No other baleen whale has so many hairs and such long ones. They are widely scattered over the head and jaws instead of being in only a few places. This is a definitely "primitive" characteristic. It is a reminder of the time when the whale had hair over all its body.

After I had returned to America and had written my book about the gray whales, I more or less forgot them. But six years ago they came to life in my mind once more. Dr. Carl Hubbs of the Scripps Institution of Oceanography, at La Jolla, California, wrote me a letter. He said the gray whales had returned to their old haunts in the Mexican lagoons. He was studying them.

He had posted students on the roof of the Institution. With a telescope they counted the number of whales that passed a given point. Two hundred were listed in the daytime from December, 1946, to February, 1947.

Then Dr. Hubbs got a Coast Guard airplane to take him south. In the lagoon where Scammon had hunted he counted 101 gray whales. Finally he organized a real expedition. They collected a yacht, fast motor boats, one helicopter and five airplanes.

They got surprising results. At the mouth of San Ignacio Lagoon the surf was pounding over sand bars. But the central channel runs far into the desert. It was dotted with whales. Many were females. Always the mothers kept their babies on their right sides. The helicopter hovered ten or fifteen feet above them. That threw the calves into a panic. They dashed from side to side. Each mother tried to shield her child with her own body.

At first the old whales were only frightened. After a while they became angry. They churned the water into foam, lashing out with their flukes. Dr. Hubbs saw why the animal was called "devilfish" by the New England whalers. The helicopter annoyed the gray whales for a week while photographers got pictures. Then the devilfish began to attack the boats of turtle fishermen. Before, they had let them alone.

When the gray whales first reappeared on the California coast, they gave the United States Navy quite

The helicopter threw the gray whales into a panic.

a scare. Constant reports came of submarines. The delicate sonar instruments registered all sorts of strange noises. Whether they were made by the devilfish is not certain. Probably they were. But in future study, scientists may be able to discover how whales talk to each other.

The gray whale is now protected by international laws. Thus far the laws are being respected. I hope this continues to be so. The devilfish give a priceless opportunity for study. No other large whale comes into shallow bays. The young are born and nursed and grow where they can be studied. All the private whale life goes on before one's eyes. Other large species live at sea, far from human knowledge.

The California lagoons are ideal open-air laboratories. Here the animals have come of their own free wills. With modern methods, we can find out many things about all whales. The knowledge will be exact, not guesswork.

Should the devilfish again be driven from their breeding grounds, they may never return. Science would be a heavy loser.

11.

A Strange Giant of the Ocean

No animal that lives in the ocean has been more important to mankind than the sperm whale. Sperm candles and oil lighted the houses of the world for decades. And throughout the ages men have marveled at this strange beast spawned in the sea.

It is the largest of the toothed whales. An old bull sperm may reach seventy feet in length. Its head is enormous and rectangular in shape. It occupies one-third of the entire body. The long, narrow lower jaw carries twenty to forty huge conical teeth. These fit into sockets in the upper jaw. In the sockets a few teeth still exist, but they are small and of no use to the animal. Probably a million years ago the upper teeth were as big as the lower. But since they were not needed, they have almost disappeared.

Quite often the lower jaw of a sperm is injured when the whale is young. As the animal grows, its jaw becomes twisted like an enormous corkscrew. The wide, spreading back part of the jaw is called "panbone." From it the old-time sailors made walking sticks, pie markers, hairpins and carvings. Etching or drawing upon the whale's teeth also helped sailors to pass the time. This was called "scrimshawing." Some of the work is very fine.

The sperm is a slate-gray whale with only a little white about the lower jaw and snout. But its great head is crisscrossed with long white scars. Sometimes splashes of white mark the belly.

A number of small throat grooves show just below the angle of the jaw. The body is not smooth, as in other whales, but has a wavy surface. A prominent hump is in the position of the back fin of fin whales.

Unlike the baleen whales, the male sperm whale is

very much larger than the female.

The upper part of the head contains an immense tank filled with liquid oil known as "spermaceti." You can cut an opening in this case and dip out ten or fifteen barrels of oil with a bucket. Spermaceti hardens slightly when cooled. Then it looks like soft white paraffin. Beneath the case is a great mass of cellular tissue. This is called the "junk." It also contains spermaceti but not in a liquid condition. Until recently spermaceti was used for oiling fine pieces of machinery. Years ago it made the very best candles.

No one knows just what use the spermaceti case is to the whale. There are many theories. Possibly it acts as a reserve food supply. The whale may draw upon it in times of food scarcity. Seals, bears and other animals store up great quantities of fat on their bodies. Because of this they are able to live without food during hibernation. Some sperms are "dry." That is, they have little oil in the blubber or case. They are always thin.

Spermaceti should not be confused with ambergris. This is a substance of value in making perfume. It is obtained only from the intestines of sick sperm whales, never from healthy ones or any other species. How it is formed is unknown. Sperms feed upon squid and cuttlefish, whose hard beaks are often found in ambergris. It may be that irritation of the intestines by these beaks has something to do with the formation of ambergris. It may be like human gallstones. Again, there are several theories.

Ambergris is light in weight. It is rarely found floating or on an ocean beach. The intestines of dead sperms have been filled with ambergris. It is black or gray in color. In perfumes its use is to make the fragrance last. It has a peculiar odor of its own, something like musk. This is as strangely pleasing to most people as catnip is to cats. If you touch it, traces of the smell remain on your hands even after several washings. For some reason you will sniff your fingers continually.

For hundreds of years ambergris has been known and used. It was supposed to be a wonderful medicine. In Asia cooks put it in certain food and wines as a spice. The Turks, particularly, considered it of great value. Pilgrims to Mecca took it as a religious offering.

Many people have brought me what they thought was ambergris, but none had the real thing. In the old days of deep-sea whaling, if a dead sperm whale was seen floating, it was investigated. The men would cut open the intestines to see if they contained ambergris.

Sperm whales often jump out of the water like humpbacks.

It was an unpleasant business. Still, some great finds were made. When ambergris was selling at twenty dollars an ounce, a Nantucket ship got 750 pounds. Since then amounts of sixty to 200 pounds have been found.

The sperm is a lover of warm currents which favor the squid and cuttlefish upon which it lives. The squid reaches a length of twenty feet or even more. The sperm sometimes has terrific battles with its prey in the dark ocean depths. The squid's arms, called tentacles, end in deadly suckers. These tear long gashes in the soft skin as they curl about the whale's head. They leave white scars crisscrossed in every direction. Most of the squid that sperms eat are not so large. They will average only three or four feet.

In Japan I took eighty yellow, parrot-like squid beaks from the stomach of one sperm whale. It also contained three enormous spiny lobsters and the remains of a shark. Sperms eat quite a good many fish at times, but they like squid best of all.

Because of its big food the sperm's throat is large. Many people asked me if the Bible story of Jonah and the whale is true. Could a man be swallowed by a whale? So I pushed my body partly down the throat of a dead sixty-foot sperm whale. I could just squeeze through. A fat man couldn't have made it. But of course a man would be dead long before he got into the stomach. The throats of baleen whales, like the sulphurbottom and others, are small, not more than seven or eight inches in diameter. That is because their food is small.

The sperm has only a single S-shaped blowhole. It is at the very end of the snout on the left side. The spout is unlike that of any other whale. It is a low, bushy column and slants forward and upward. Sperms blow much more often and more regularly than other species. I saw one spout thirty times. It was swimming very slowly during the entire breathing period. Because of this regularity, the hunters can tell just how long a sperm will be down. They know, too, where it will come up.

When the blowing is finished, the whale's head gradually sinks. Then the back appears, and the great flukes are lifted high in the air. The animal goes straight down. It will remain below for from fifteen to forty minutes. The sperm is very playful. Like the humpback it often "breaches." It leaps high in the air and falls back upon its side in a great cloud of spray.

Along the Japanese coast sperm whales appear in July. They may come in herds of 400 or 500. The great animals lie at the surface, spouting continually. The sea will be alive with whales for a mile or more. When shore whalers find a school of this sort, they signal all the vessels that may be near. Then there is excitement for everyone. The guns bang as often as they can be loaded, and the whales are made fast. The school will usually move very slowly, blowing and wallowing at the surface. The ones in the center of the herd pay no attention to those being killed on the outskirts. At times, however, the whales will stampede at the first gunshot.

At Aikawa a Japanese gunner found a herd of sperm whales. They were a long way from the village. The man let his greed get the better of his judgment. He killed ten whales and made them all fast to the ship. She could hardly move under the load. It was three days before she reached the station. The meat was all spoiled. The ten whales were not as valuable as a single fresh one would have been. The meat of the sperm is dark and full of oil. Therefore, it is of little use as food. Only the very poorest people eat it in Japan.

Every whaleman has stories to tell of "rogue" sperms. These are usually old bulls that live a solitary life. They become vicious and will turn furiously upon the boats when struck with a harpoon. Often the attacks are deliberate. Ships have been rammed and sunk by sperm whales.

British naturalists of the Discovery Committee studied sperm whales both in the sub-Antarctic and at Durban, South Africa. They found out many interesting facts about the life history of the sperms. The headquarters of sperm whales is in the tropics all over the world. But during summer in both hemispheres some seek more temperate waters. Pairing takes place during this migration. The main part of the pairing season is from August to December.

The females carry their young for sixteen months. As an average the calves are fourteen feet long at birth. Since the females are only about thirty-five feet in length, this is an unusually large baby—almost half as big as the mother. The young are nursed for six months, and the females have calves every two years like the baleen whales.

Sometimes old bulls migrate by themselves into colder waters, leaving the main herd. Probably they have been driven out by younger males. Apparently sperm whales like many wives. That doesn't seem to be true of the baleen whales. Because the males are so much larger than the females, they can easily be distinguished.

Sperms are not an important part of the whale fishery today. Only in South Africa, Chile and Japan are they hunted. The reason is because sperm oil is not suitable for refining as a food product. International laws have been passed protecting all sperm whales under thirty-five feet. Thus the cows will be safe since few are over that length. Probably the animals will become fairly abundant again as time goes on.

The beaked, or ziphioid, whales make a strange and

interesting family of toothed whales. All except one are exceedingly rare. Some are known only from a single specimen. No members of this family have a notch in the outer edge of the flukes. They bear one or two pairs of teeth in the lower jaw, near or at the end. These sometimes develop in an unusual way.

The front portion of the skull of all the beaked whales is a long cylinder of very hard bone. Because it is so solid, this part of the skull fossilizes perfectly. When digging for the fortifications about the city of Antwerp, scientists found hundreds of these bones and teeth buried in the rocks. Also many have been taken from the Red Crag deposits in England.

Beaked whales are evidently an ancient group that was widely distributed at one time. Today they are found most often in the seas about New Zealand and Australia. But single specimens are continually appearing unexpectedly in almost every ocean of the world. Their habits are virtually unknown.

One of this group used to be of commercial importance. That is the bottlenose whale. It is about thirty feet long and is the largest member. It is fairly common in the North Atlantic where it was hunted for its oil. It eats squid as do other members of the family.

12.

Porpoises and Dolphins

Many of you must have seen porpoises leaping about in the ocean. Often they will follow a boat, swimming close beside the bow. These animals are really toothed whales although we call them porpoises. There are perhaps a hundred kinds of porpoises found in all the oceans of the world. Four kinds go into fresh water. Some of them have pointed snouts. These are usually called dolphins to distinguish them from the round-headed porpoises. But I prefer to speak of them all as porpoises.

Then there won't be confusion with the fish that is properly named dolphin. It is, of course, impossible to write about all the porpoises in this book. So I have selected only a few of the most interesting ones as examples.

The largest member of the family is the terrible killer whale. It reaches a length of thirty feet. The mouth is armed with great curved teeth in both jaws. A killer can always be known, even at a distance, by its very high, slender dorsal fin. This stands up six feet in the male, but the female has a fin of only three or four feet. The color is black, but with a big trident-shaped white area on the throat and belly. Just behind the eyes are white oval spots. No other whale is colored like that.

Killers are the wolves of the sea. They hunt in packs of five to twenty individuals. Only the great sperm whale is safe from their attacks. They will eat anything that swims. Fish, birds, seals, walruses, and porpoises go down their throats. They can hold an unbelievable amount of food. There is a record of thirteen porpoises and fourteen seals taken from the stomach of a twenty-one-foot killer. The beasts live in all oceans from the Arctic to the Antarctic.

They hunt more in bays than in the open sea because there they find much to eat. They can swim at tremendous speed. Their great strength and savage nature terrify other animals.

One distinguished scientist told me a story that illustrates this fact. On an island in the Bering Sea he was collecting sea lions for a museum. He had shot three or four. The sea lions rushed toward the water in terror. Suddenly the high dorsal fin of a killer appeared just offshore. The sea lions stopped short and would not leave the beach. They preferred to face the unknown danger on land rather than certain death in the water. From the time they were born they had been taught by their mothers to stay away from killer whales.

Captain Scammon says that killers frighten even a full-grown walrus. If a female walrus is swimming with a pup, the little one will climb on its mother's back for safety. Then the killer dives. It comes up under the walrus and dumps the baby into the water. Instantly the little one is seized and devoured.

I have told how the killers so terrify the California gray whale that it becomes paralyzed with fright. And how the savage beasts eat out the whale's tongue!

Captain Scott writes a remarkable story about killers. His ship was moored to an ice floe in the Antarctic. Two Eskimo dogs were tied near the edge. Captain

Scott saw six or seven killers swimming about excitedly. He called to Ponting, the photographer, to get pictures of the whales. Ponting ran to the margin of the floe. Suddenly the killers disappeared. The next moment the whole floe heaved up and split into pieces. Captain Scott says he could hear the booming noise as the whales rose under the ice and struck it with their backs.

Ponting leaped to safety. By chance the splits were between the dogs so neither fell into the water. The whales appeared to be astonished. Their heads shot up through the cracks they had made. Captain Scott could see their small glistening eyes and the terrible array of teeth as they looked around. After this they left.

Scott says he had known that the killers would snap up a man if he fell into the water. But he never thought the animals could break ice, two and a half feet thick, or that they would act together.

Another remarkable member of the porpoise family is the narwhal. It is a twelve-foot spotted whale that lives in the Arctic Ocean. In the male two of the front teeth have developed into long, forward-projecting tusks. One is usually much bigger than the other. I have a narwhal tusk in my study that measures six feet. Admiral Peary gave it to me.

The tusk of a narwhal may be as much as six feet long.

An animal called the "unicorn" was supposed to have lived in ancient times. It had a spirally twisted horn projecting from its forehead. Of course it was a mythical creature. But how did the idea start? Perhaps in prehistoric times some sailors saw a narwhal sticking its tusk up at the edge of the ice. They came home and told the story. So it went down by word of mouth in tradition.

Another porpoise, known as the white whale, is a relative of the narwhal. They are put together in a separate sub-family. The white whale is a northern species, too. But during the spring, before the Arctic ice opens, it comes into the St. Lawrence River. There, it is killed for its very fine jaw oil. Also the skin makes excellent leather.

Years ago, I went to the little town of Tadousac, Quebec, to collect specimens for the American Museum of Natural History. Some of the French-Canadian natives along the river made their living by hunting white whales. I was with three of them on their sailboat. They could not speak a single word of English. We went to sleep in a tiny cabin on the boat.

Next morning I was awakened by the regular *lap, lap, lap* of water. I knew we had started down the river. Crawling from my narrow shelf, I wriggled through the hatchway on to the deck. It was a perfect morning, bright and warm. We were headed for an island four miles away. There, twenty or thirty white whales were feeding on fish. They darted back and forth after the skipping capelin. I was greatly excited, for I was to try my luck at shooting a whale.

When the canoe was in the water, we slid away from the sailboat with hardly a sound. I sat in front. Beside me rested a heavy shotgun loaded with a lead ball. On my right lay a slender harpoon. The line was neatly coiled and fastened to a big cedar float.

We had only a few hundred yards to paddle. In a

few minutes we were right among the whales. On every side sounded the short, metallic puffs as they blew. Young animals in the school were brown. They remain so for the first year and then change to snowy white.

We drifted quietly among them, waiting to pick our specimen. They were so intent on feeding that they paid no attention to us. Finally a big white fellow slipped under water and headed directly for us. Up he came with a rush and down again. So close he was, that I could see the water run in little ripples off his pure white back. My fingers trembled on the trigger of the gun. But he was still coming toward us. I wanted him as close as possible. In a few seconds a patch of green water began to smooth out right in front. I fired the instant the snowy head appeared above the surface.

The porpoise thrashed about as I grabbed the harpoon. At the thrust of the iron, the animal threw itself high in the air, falling back in a cloud of spray. It made a wild rush to one side and again the ghostly form shot from the water.

The porpoise fought desperately to free itself. It rushed from side to side, and our canoe backed off. We had thrown the float overboard at the first leap. Finally the animal's struggles became less violent. It was having a hard time staying upright. Then I fired a second ball into its neck. It turned over and slowly sank. We paddled for the buoy which was bobbing about near us and took it aboard. The porpoise was brought to the surface by forcing the canoe ahead.

It was beached in a sandy cove. The gray rock wall rose in a jagged mass above the water. It made a striking background for the pure white body. But the beautiful creature, a very spirit of the Arctic, seemed strangely out of place. It should have been on a field of ice.

Not a single shade of color tinged the body except for the outer margin of the flukes. There a narrow line was grayish-brown. The small head, unlike that of most whales, joined the body by a distinct neck. It ended in a short stubby snout or lip. Each jaw carried nine rather weak teeth.

We remained at the island for three days and killed two more whales. The Frenchmen took the oil and hides. I got the skeletons and plaster casts.

One of the most common porpoises on our Atlantic coast is the bottlenose. For two hundred years a "fishery" for these animals was carried on at Cape Hatteras, North Carolina. The porpoises were valuable because of their jaw oil, hides and blubber. At the base of each jawbone is a blob of fat. This gives a fine oil. It was used for watches, clocks and delicate machines. The rather tough hide, like that of the white whale, could be tanned for leather. It made the very best razor strops.

The bottlenose porpoises are regular winter visitors to Cape Hatteras. Schools continually pass just outside the line of surf. The "fishermen" would string a 1000-foot net parallel to the breakers. When porpoises swam between it and shore, the ends were closed and it was dragged onto the beach. Forty or fifty animals might be trapped at one time.

A few years ago at the Marine Studios in Florida, several bottlenose porpoises were caught. They were captured in an inlet by means of a long net. One of them was about two years old. He weighed 150 pounds and was six feet long. He was given the name "Flippy."

Many experiments were tried on Flippy in an effort to find out how intelligent porpoises are. It was shown that the bottlenose has a rather high level of intelligence. It is between the dog and the chimpanzee.

Flippy has been taught to do many amazing tricks. One is to raise himself out of water and pull a rubber ball. This rings a bell, and he gets a fish as a reward.

Flippy the porpoise has learned to do many tricks.

He will swim through an underwater hoop. After a long time, he was taught to jump through a hoop three feet above the water.

Most amazing of all, Flippy learned to wear a harness and tow a surfboard like a motorboat. Sometimes a dog rides alone on the surfboard; sometimes he rides with a girl.

Scientists at the Marine Studios have learned a great deal about porpoises from those in their own pool. Much of the information applies equally well to all the cetacea

One of them is to tow a surfboard like a motorboat.

including the big whales. They discovered that porpoises can make very distinct sounds under water that are definitely a means of communication. These have been described as "jaw clapping, whistling, chirping, squeaking, and the drawn-out grating noise of a rusty hinge." The scientists also watched a porpoise give birth to her young and saw the mother nurse her baby and care for it like any land mammal.

I regret to end this book. Writing about whales has

again brought back to me the intense interest of their study. You see them for only a few brief moments above the surface. Then they are gone, and you wonder what goes on down in the depths of the ocean. But little by little, naturalists are finding out. The modern undersea instruments are opening a new world to us who float on the water in ships. Some of the dwellers in that new world are whales. Every year we learn a little more of their private lives. All of it is fascinating.

Index

Index

Index

Index